STEALING

HARPER'S
MAGAZINE
PRESS

How America's Employees

STEALING

Are Stealing Their Companies Blind

By Mark Lipman

Edited and with an Introduction by Robert Daley,
former Deputy Commissioner,
New York City Police Department

HARPER'S MAGAZINE PRESS
Published in Association with Harper & Row
New York

"Harper's" is the registered trademark of Harper & Row, Publishers, Inc.

STEALING *Copyright* © 1973 by Robert Daley. *All rights reserved. Printed in the United States of America. No part of this book may be used or reproduced in any manner whatsoever without written permission except in the case of brief quotations embodied in critical articles and reviews. For information address Harper & Row, Publishers, Inc., 10 East 53rd Street, New York, N.Y. 10022. Published simultaneously in Canada by Fitzhenry & Whiteside Limited, Toronto.*

FIRST EDITION

STANDARD BOOK NUMBER: 06–126342–7

LIBRARY OF CONGRESS CATALOG CARD NUMBER: 72–81473

Designed by Sidney Feinberg

Contents

Introduction

by ROBERT DALEY,
former Deputy Commissioner,
New York City Police Department

At this point I know something about crime, and I subscribe to the opinion, shared by others within the criminal justice system, that America today is caught in a crime wave that is both far more extensive and far more of a threat to the life of the nation than most people suspect. I am not talking only about the increase in murders in New York or about petty shoplifting in Kansas. I'm talking about systematic stealing. I have been out there in the streets of New York and in the streets of Squaresville, U.S.A., too, and I have seen it firsthand in both places, and I am as astonished by the ingenuity of American thieves as I am by their greed. Most of all I am astonished by their multitude. They are everywhere—they are all around us. Although a proportion of them are stickup men, burglars, and such against whom the police can act, the vast majority are insiders—men inside stores and factories, who are believed by those around them to be "trusted" employees. Such thieves range in rank from assembly-line workers to executives. The only thing they have in common is their rapacity. They are engaged in the systematic looting of the premises and thus, in effect, of the system under which we all live.

Let me tell you about Mark Lipman, a private investigator who employs about eighty agents, conducts about sixty cases at once, and who works from coast to coast, principally in department stores and factories. Let me tell you also about a major department store chain, owner of one department store in downtown Dallas, one central warehouse, and six other department stores in suburban Dallas shopping centers.

Between March, 1969, and Christmas, 1971, Lipman conducted seven different investigations in one or another of those stores. Each investigation began because management suspected that large-scale stealing was going on in that particular store. Each time one or more of Lipman's undercover agents went to work in that store. Each investigation lasted about two months. The agent sent back to Lipman the names of the employees he had seen steal, or who had bragged of stealing, or who were reputed to steal regularly. As soon as Lipman felt he had enough evidence, whether hearsay or otherwise, to be reasonably sure of who was guilty, he himself went into the store and interrogated those implicated, one after the other. Within a few minutes he usually obtained each suspect's confession, and within a few minutes after that a detailed statement signed by the suspect and witnessed by both Lipman and management.

End of that particular case.

Well, no.

All of these stores are interconnected on many levels. Trucks, goods, and people go back and forth between them every day. One can assume that Lipman's activities in one store were known instantly in all the others. After each case, talk about Lipman and the thieves he bagged must have gone on for days.

But the stealing hardly even slowed down.

The case Lipman broke on September 11, 1969, involved a ring of fourteen people. They were getting merchandise out of one of the suburban branches in hampers that they pushed onto the truck which each day came to deliver food to the store cafeteria. I have the signed statements before me:

"In the past three years I have averaged taking about 10 cases of lady's Palizzio shoes per month with about 25 pairs of shoes to the case. This is equal to 6,000 pairs of shoes worth about $150,000. I have taken about 1,100 pair of men's pants and blue jeans averaging $15 per pair, or $16,500. I have taken socks, shirts, radios, Polaroid cameras, a case of Adams Hats only last week. . . . The total amount of the merchandise mentioned in this statement, retail value, is $188,100."

". . . I started taking merchandise from the dock into my car. . . . I started taking ladies' dresses out in January 1968 and during this 80-week period I would steal a rod of dresses per time and average a rod of dresses every other week at 65 dresses to a rod, or 2,600 dresses. . . . The dresses retailed for $104,000 total. . . . there were four of us in on the dress transactions. . . . I have taken out on an average 25 men's suits a month or about 825 men's suits. . . . these averaged retail $110 each or $90,750. . . . About three weeks ago I got 19 radios. . . . the total amount of merchandise mentioned in this statement, retail value, is $203,080."

". . . I also put three TV's in a hamper this morning. (Name) pushed the hamper to the dock and (Second Name) put the TV's in (Third Name's) truck. . . . The total amount of the merchandise mentioned in this statement is $95,900."

The total dollar amount which the suspects admitted stealing came to about half a million dollars, and the company later recovered $200,000 from its insurance company. A good deal of merchandise was also recovered from the suspects' homes.

What happened to the fourteen thieves?

The police entered the case and were given copies of the

signed confessions. Criminal charges were eventually brought against two of the fourteen, who, after pleading guilty, were released by the court on probation.

Less than two months later, in the same suburban store, Lipman caught the manager of the housekeeping department, who was in the habit of borrowing money from his subordinates. The swindle worked this way. The manager would borrow, say, $25 from a worker, then juggle the time cards so that the worker would be credited that week with $30 worth of overtime. The manager never had to pay back his loans; the workers involved made a profit. It was a lovely setup unless you happened to own stock in the store.

Six months later, in the chain's main warehouse, Lipman caught eight men who admitted having stolen, inside of a few months, over $62,000 worth of company merchandise.

None of the other thieves caught by Lipman in those stores, about 49 people in the seven cases, were ever prosecuted.

"We did not stop the stealing in those stores," Lipman said later. "We never stopped the stealing. But how can you stop the stealing in America today when thieves know that even if caught they are not going to get more than a pat on the wrist? Thieves know that. They're not stupid."

Why did the Dallas police never prosecute?

Because the principal thieves were married men with children and no previous criminal record; because they didn't seem vicious enough to prosecute. Because, although they stole vast amounts, they got very little money themselves—fences paid them 20 percent or less of the actual value. They got cheated, they hardly seemed smart enough to prosecute, one almost felt sorry for them. Because although America is terrified of violent crime, it prefers to believe that other crime—grand larceny, for instance—either doesn't exist or isn't important, or both.

The Dallas police have the same problems we have in New York. Jails are jammed, and besides, each criminal exits from them a harder and more dangerous man than when he went in. The courts are jammed; they are clotted with cases. By the time a case comes to trial, the witnesses have forgotten their testimony or can't be found. In addition, the safeguards of our constitutional system are so strict that it is always extremely difficult to get a conviction in a jury trial. A jury very likely would not consider that these department store thieves had done society any real harm. The store was insured, wasn't it?

And so the Dallas police, like the police in all major cities today, think of crime in categories. They concentrate on certain categories, leaving little manpower for others. We do the same in New York.

In New York last year about 100,000 cars were stolen. A good many of the rings that stole them were broken by our detectives. In one particular case, I was personally involved. The two ringleaders, I learned, had already that year been arrested for car theft a total of six times. After each arrest they were released on bail to await trial, and while out on bail, our investigation proved, they simply stole more cars. Detectives get frustrated by such nasty details, and they howl, as I did, when interviewed on TV. But the feeling of the community seems to be that such crooks are not really dangerous to society and that there is no urgency to put them behind bars. The cars stolen were of course insured, were they not?

But perhaps the time has come in this country to treat crime as crime, to arrest and prosecute all wrongdoers, whatever the category, and to deal with them in the courts promptly and severely.

At present, so much is being stolen from the nation's factories and stores that all of us are paying $100 for a suit that should only have cost $75. How much worse do we want it to get? Somebody has to pay for the merchandise going out the back door. That somebody is you and me.

The basic problem is that most citizens do not know, and they do not want to know, about merchandise going out the back door.

There are, you might say, standup crooks. The stickup man, for instance, comes in behind a gun, takes what he wants, and leaves. Standup crooks can be dealt with, more or less, by the police, and they also get priority treatment in the courts, and they go to jail regularly and for long enough terms.

There are also sneak crooks with whom the police can't deal because the police don't know they're there. No one knows they're there. These individuals steal a regular amount of goods or money or services day after day without anyone's knowing it, working either alone or with colleagues, and they are never unmasked until such time as the business is about to go bankrupt. Their very existence is signaled, in most cases, by the company auditor who suddenly notices a steady and alarming drop in profits. At this point the boss, in panic, in hysteria sometimes, calls in private investigators to find out what has gone wrong. He calls private investigators because the crime is taking place not on the street, which in effect is the only place where the police patrol, but inside of the place he owns, by men to whom he has given the tools with which to rob him. He has as yet no evidence on which the police can act. There is as yet no evidence at all.

Enter the private detective. The agent whom Lipman used to break the half-million dollar case in Dallas in September, 1969, was named Billy Tucker. He was black and had a crippled foot. "That's an asset in a job like this," said Lipman. "No one suspects a man with a crippled foot of being a detective."

The police departments of the country use undercover agents at times. But each agent is also a cop, which means that he can have no abnormalities or deformities of any kind, and that he can operate only within his own city or jurisdiction, where he is to a greater or lesser extent known and therefore recognizable. Whereas often a man like Lipman will hire a professional tailor, or a professional surveyor, or a professional auditor, train him as an agent and then plant him next to the suspected thieves in some other city. The police departments of this country can't do that. They operate under civil service laws. They are unable under the law to go out and get the specific agent they want, swear him in as a cop, and plant him. He must come up through the ranks like everybody else.

The police, when it comes time for an interrogation, are obliged to warn suspects of their rights and to produce a lawyer or lawyers for them. The district attorney must be called. The police can offer no deals to induce a confession; only the D.A. can. Lie detector tests are almost never used.

The private investigator, however, operating on much less evidence than it would take to win a conviction in court, can confront the suspect, throw damning evidence at him, and accuse him to his face, all within seconds. The shock value of this is often great enough to induce a confession.

No force is used. There are no tricks. The interrogator has only surprise and knowledge on his side. The suspect, shocked and guilty, blurts out the truth.

Civil libertarians will scream that such tactics are unconstitutional. Not so. And anyway, where did the notion come from in this country that the guilty must be protected from all risk—all risk—of self-incrimination?

And while on the subject of civil liberties, let's talk of another of the chief weapons of private investigators, the polygraph or lie detector. Private investigators use this instrument as a matter of course—I have watched them do it—and they tend to accept the results as 100 percent accurate. Specifically, they immediately release any suspect that the instrument exonerates, informing management that said suspect is guiltless. The instrument, in effect, saves them countless hours of investigation and frees them to concentrate on the guilty.

The police can compel no one to take a polygraph examination, and the results are not accepted in court anyway. Private investigators, on the other hand, can ask management to "suggest" that a suspected thief take the test. His refusal is not supposed to endanger his job, but this is a real world, isn't it? I'm all for the use of the polygraph where wrongdoing is solidly suspected. Its indiscriminate use in screening job applicants, however, is quite another thing.

The polygraph is three instruments in one. It measures rate of breathing, blood pressure/heart beat, and the amount of sweat secreted by the fingertips. When a man lies, all three of these instruments register abrupt changes, and these changes are marked on graphs. Confronted by the graphs, the guilty man often confesses, and when he does so he usually adds details that the polygraph instrument, which can measure only yes or no answers, could not have produced itself.

So, again, private detectives have at their command tools which are denied the police.

It is rare enough to hear a police official praise private detectives and their techniques, and I should hasten to add that the only one I know personally and have watched work is Lipman. However, there must be others out there who are as careful and as dedicated as he is. I saw nothing reprehensible in his methods or their effects, which where to catch dishonest employees for a fee, and the reason I am praising the whole idea of private detectives in industry is that the criminal justice system alone can no longer cope with crime in this country. According to a recent statement by the Insurance Information Institute, company losses from embezzlement, pilfering, and outright theft by employees have soared to $10 million per day, more than $3 billion a year. These losses are more than nationwide street robbery and burglary losses combined.

It is the Insurance Information Institute's estimate that company losses will double in the next decade—that would be $6 billion per year in stolen goods floating around without a shot being fired or a gun even shown.

There is just too much crime in America today and the criminal justice system is too small, too antiquated, too unresponsive to the changing needs of society. It is clogged. The oil has congealed, and so the machine starts with painful slowness each time and then stops of its own accord before each job is done.

We in the criminal justice system need help. We need help urgently, and the only place we can get it is from the private sector. We all ought to be living in a society where public law enforcement could cope with all crime, but we are not and it cannot, and this is especially true in the small towns with their small isolated groups of virtually untrained gun-carrying policemen capable of operating speed traps, and that's about all.

At a recent security conference held by the trucking industry in a New York City hotel, Mayor John V. Lindsay declared: "Our society makes its best gain where the private sector and the public sector come together. Crime, whether it occurs at the end of the Chicago Thruway, or at Logan Airport in Boston, or on the San Francisco waterfront, whether it's a robbery in the Bronx—crime is too important to be left solely to government to solve."

More and more, it is *not* being left to government to solve, and the most booming business in the country seems to be the security business. Atlanta has had an increase of 2,000 security guards in the last four years. One Chicago detective agency has increased business 40 percent since 1969. New York's largest guard service has grown into a vast enterprise grossing $134.6 million per year. Detroit now has 107 firms supplying more guards to businesses and apartment houses than the city has on its 5,200 man police force. Mark Lipman himself, a private investigator since 1935, decided to start a guards business with his son Ira about ten years ago. They called it Guardsmark. It is already the sixth largest guards firm in the country, with over four thousand guards and with offices coast to coast. Most times, when Lipman breaks a case, he will advise management that more security is needed in their plant, that stealing there is too easy. Too often, management declines to do so. They seem to think that what Lipman has just uncovered is some sort of isolated phenomenon.

It is no isolated phenomenon, unfortunately.

The police are catching more stickup men and muggers than ever before, and the private investigators are catching more trusted employees than ever before. When the cops are called in time and the stickup man lies dead on the doorstep and is carried away in a body bag while a dozen flashbulbs pop, you read about it. You rarely read about the other kind of crime because the hysterical employer who at last hires private investigators and who, aghast, listens to their report, is by this time so embarrassed that he is not about to tell anybody what has happened. Sometimes (not always) the private investigators advise him to prosecute. Most often he won't do it. He is satisfied to fire the thief, or the ring of thieves, believing that with this act he has cleaned out his plant. Afterwards he wants only to go on with business as usual. He pays the bill, and considers himself saved. In a few weeks, however, new thieves with new tricks move in on him. Meanwhile, the original thief moves on somewhere else and robs some other store or factory blind.

I have been in mid-America and watched this and much else happen. I've also had to deal with crime in New York. The two have little in common except that both are on an incredible upsurge. I judge this as evidence that a new morality exists in America, one which preaches to workers to get away with whatever they think they can get away with, to steal if the joint isn't locked up tight, to terrorize factory owner's who suddenly find that after a lifetime in business, they are suddenly about to go under.

I have concluded that only family background, environment, and opportunity decide whether an individual thief will steal with a gun, or by altering an invoice, by casually tossing a box of goods onto a garbage truck that an accomplice is about to drive out of the factory gates or by holding a knife at a pedestrian's neck.

Last year, because I was curious about his methods, I went with Lipman into a furniture plant, into a number of clothing factories, and into a meat-packing plant that had just done fifteen million pounds worth of business in a single month without earning a dime profit. As Lipman exposed the thieves in each place, I found myself suffering with more than one owner as he realized what had been done to him and for how long. And I worried about what the future holds for America. It is one thing to believe that in a place like New York stickup men abound. It is another to realize that out there in quiet, safe and sane Squaresville, stealing is just as rampant. There may be less violence, and therefore less terror, but the decayed morality is the same. In both places the future of America is in doubt.

I went into no automobile plants during that tour. Obviously, no employee can walk out of such a place with an entire car over his shoulder. Somebody would notice. But I daresay Ford, and General Motors and the rest have a shrinking inventory of about the same proportions as that of the meat-packing plant, and the clothing factories. I imagine Ford and General Motors have hired some very busy private detectives lately. I also imagine that they, like the meat-packing plant, are not a bit anxious to brag about what the private detectives have found.

A good deal of New York street crime is committed by addicts high on drugs. Theoretically we could eliminate most such crime if we could solve the drug problem. In other words, drug-related crime is peculiar to this time and this place. It is comprehensible. Similarly, most other violent street crime is committed by young ghetto blacks. It too is comprehensible. It is committed out of hatred for the white establishment and to get money. Stickup men and muggers don't work for a living. If we could solve ghetto poverty, if we could provide meaningful jobs, we could no doubt eliminate most stickups.

But the people who are looting the factories and department stores of this nation are not addicts and are not the ghetto poor. They are men who work for a living, and they steal only on the side. They steal vast amounts without making larceny in any way a career. They come in all colors and all ages. Many are well educated. Many are religious. Some earn less than $2 an hour. Some on the executive level earn $30,000 a year or more. The only difference between the worker and the executive as thief is opportunity, and the executive steals more faster and over longer periods of time.

Let me tell you about a recent case in New York. Two of our plainclothes patrolmen, Arthur Esposito and Joseph Fox, were strolling through the garment district at 10:15 in the morning when they spied two men, brothers, whom they recognized as having been arrested previously for truck larcenies. The two plainclothesmen, trying to appear inconspicuous, sauntered along behind the brothers. They trailed them less than a block. On 39th Street between Sixth and Seventh avenues, one of the brothers, Raymond Berry, 26, walked up to a double-parked truck, saw that it was unoccupied, stepped to the back, took a wrench out of his belt, snapped the lock, and opened the doors. The second brother, Alhern Melvin Berry, approached with a hand truck and loaded four cartons of textiles onto his hand truck. The two patrolmen could have arrested the brothers then and there, but they chose not to. Instead they followed the brothers and the hand truck across Seventh Avenue through the traffic, along 39th Street to Eighth Avenue, and then down Eighth and into a loft building on 38th Street.

The two plainclothesmen got on the same elevator with the brothers. All four stepped off on the eighth floor. As the brothers pushed the hand truck around a corner in the corridor, the two cops dropped back a little. The brothers entered an office marked Roguel Textile Firm. The cops approached the door and listened. Inside, the brothers were bargaining with the fence.

At this point the cops pushed their way in. The alleged fence, one Edward Hines, 50, was looking through the stolen goods. Suddenly the door opened, and in came Ernest Bendano, 57. He had four rolls of textiles to sell. They were stolen. The cops locked up all four men. The Berry brothers were charged with grand larceny, with possession of burglary tools, and with possession of stolen property.

Hines was charged with possession of stolen property and with criminal receiving of stolen property. Bendano was charged with possession of stolen property. An estimated $100,000 worth of stolen goods was recovered.

Great police work, you say, to nab all four like that. But wait, the story isn't over. It was found that Raymond Berry, though only 26 years old, had twenty-seven previous arrests for grand larceny, burglary, and narcotics crimes. He had already been convicted sixteen times. Eight other cases were pending.

His brother Alhern had thirty-one previous arrests and could boast twelve convictions since 1968, with seven cases pending. A bench warrant was out for his arrest in connection with another case.

What were such men doing still strolling the streets, you ask? Good question. Naturally such obviously professional criminals were promptly, you say, put behind bars and are still there. Not so. Alhern Berry was released on $2,500 bail, and Raymond Berry was released on $3,000 bail.

This was three months ago as I write, and they are still out on bail, turned loose by the overloaded American criminal justice system. They are awaiting trial. They are waiting for the system to get around to them. And if they should choose to pass the time by breaking into a few trucks, I can't imagine that anyone would be too surprised.

The alleged fence, Hines, was released on $5,000 bail. Bendano went free on parole.

At about the same time Hines and Bendano were set free in New York, Lipman was working in a suburb of Los Angeles, in a major carpet mill which was losing entire rolls of carpeting. Two of his undercover agents were trying to develop leads inside the plant, and four more were tailing suspects as they left the plant at night.

Nothing was being hijacked. There was no hint of violence. The thief (or thieves) was destroying invoices so that carpeting which left the plant legally and normally in effect disappeared —nobody got billed for it. Who was destroying the paperwork? Who was he working for?

The company auditor came forward with the name of a wholesale carpet company, call it the CBA Company. This company had formerly bought vast amounts of carpeting from the mill; now it bought only scraps, and it paid cash.

But this firm was prosperous. It had a net worth of over half a million dollars. It owned various trade names and a retail outlet in Los Angeles.

Within the client's carpet mill, there were six people who might be destroying the invoices. Lipman's men tailed them all. They staked out CBA's retail store, and they began to run background checks on the CBA people and also on the six suspects.

Almost immediately one of the suspects was found to have a criminal record, and as surveillance was concentrated on him, he was seen to enter CBA's retail store regularly. Eventually a leased truck full of the carpet mill's merchandise pulled up at this store. Lipman's men saw the prime suspect unload it.

Proper invoices for this merchandise were found to exist.

Lipman's agents watched the suspect at work all the next day, watched him strolling in and out of the client's data processing office, apparently trying to find the invoices and destroy them. Some copies he did destroy.

When Lipman felt that he had as much evidence against this man as he was likely to get, he ordered the suspect into the president's office and interrogated him. Under severe questioning by Lipman, the man cracked.

He admitted that another factory employee had been helping him destroy the paper work, and that this had been going on for eighteen months. He admitted that the most he ever earned for a shipment of stolen carpeting was $200, that many times he got nothing, and that sometimes he got $100. He admitted that the average shipment was worth up to $2,000, for only the best carpeting was stolen. He admitted that the total value of the carpeting he had helped steal came to $312,000.

He declared that larceny on this scale was never his idea, but rather the idea of the CBA officials, and he was believed, partly because he got so little money out of it, but mostly because his story checked out on a subsequent polygraph test. He used to moonlight for the CBA Company, he said. Officials there had found out about his criminal record and threatened to have him fired if he did not agree to help them loot his employers. Once, when he wanted to back out, a CBA official stuck a gun in his face and threatened to kill him.

The suspect signed a statement attesting to all this. A second suspect whom he had implicated was interrogated by Lipman, confessed, and signed a similar statement.

So Lipman proved that one solvent company was robbing its chief supplier to the tune of $312,000 (possibly much more) over a period of at least eighteen months.

As this is written, there has been no criminal prosecution in this case, neither of the two former mill employees nor of the CBA officials.

Lipman went away, his job concluded.

At the request of the carpet mill, two of Lipman's undercover agents were left behind because they had uncovered evidence of narcotics selling within the mill, and before too long the local police did make some narcotics arrests. The undercover agents have since testified in this narcotics trial and convictions were obtained. Which has nothing to do with grand larceny—nothing to do with $312,000 worth of stolen carpeting.

Grand larceny is not something that this country is uptight about at this time. Narcotics yes, larceny no.

For the most part, the country doesn't even know so much grand larceny is even going on.

Which, obviously, is part of the reason so much of it is.

The Mark Lipmans of this country can do no more than they are already doing. No doubt Lipman is unhappy about what he sees every day but he has no voice in the nation's councils. He could protest a little if he wanted, he could scream a bit, but nobody important would hear him.

The police departments of this country are not happy either. However, they could in fact do more than they are doing because they do have a voice, and if they screamed more often and more loudly, people sooner or later might listen.

This is the principal reason I have written this Introduction. It's a form of screaming. Listen to me. Listen to us. This is what is going on in this country today. Do you want it to continue this way? Do you want it, in all likelihood, to get worse?

If not, you must be willing to pay the cost of redesigning the entire criminal justice system, and that cost will be high. The corrections departments of the nation must be rebuilt along modern lines. The court system must be rebuilt. Our current jails are not only overfull, they brutalize people, and so judges and juries are reluctant to send men there for anything except the most heinous crimes. The result: the Berry brothers of New York with their combined record of fifty-eight previous arrests are sent out onto the street again to while away the months before trial. Two of the men who looted that Dallas department store chain of half a million dollars, though pleading guilty, are released on probation, and the others are not prosecuted at all. The officials of the CBA Carpet Company in Los Angeles are not prosecuted.

I am not arguing for preventive detention but for swift trials. There should be enough prosecutors, enough defense lawyers, enough courtrooms so that every person arrested comes to trial within a week, except in exceptional cases. And there should be detention facilities available—warm, comfortable, reasonable facilities—in which to keep some of these suspects during that week.

There should be many kinds of penal institutions, each one designed to match the severity of a specific type of crime and also to match the personalities of the men inside it. A prisoner ought to be able to strive for promotion into a better-grade prison, and the best grade ought to be very close to freedom itself. In addition, he ought to be schooled and taught some meaningful trade every step of the way, so that society doesn't have to cope with him again the minute he comes out.

There should be enough police detectives in each state—and at the very least each state's detective forces ought to be under state control in order to facilitate investigations that cross town jurisdictions—so that when a man like Lipman uncovers evidence against the CBA Company or its equivalent, the detectives can take that evidence, which admittedly is not yet strong enough for conviction in a jury trial, and go on with the investigation until it either peters out or reaches a grand jury.

There is so much to be done.

But at present America merely talks about crime. It does nothing, and the crime wave goes on.

Most of the cases that follow took place within a three-month period last year. Mark Lipman would call me when he thought each case was about to break, and I would meet him in Chicago, or Texas, or wherever. I wanted to study his method of operation, and I did so, and I had no official capacity of any kind.

However, I had a tape recorder with me, and I taped parts of his interrogations of suspects. These tapes have no legal value in criminal court, and in any case none of the factory owners wanted to prosecute afterwards. It was my idea to include sections of these transcripts within Lipman's own accounts of the cases in question. Where indicated, these are real thieves talking, real thieves attempting to justify their conduct. And of course this is the real Lipman conducting each interrogation. Interrogation is his specialty—it is the thing he does best.

In nearly all cases, the names of the firms and people involved have been changed. This was necessary to protect the reputations of the victimized firms, to protect those suspects who proved to be not guilty, and to protect confessed thieves who, however, have never been prosecuted and convicted.

In all other respects, this book is as accurate as we could make it.

New York City
May 1972

STEALING

1. Chicago: The Meat Case

•

How to sell fifteen million pounds of meat a month at no profit whatsoever

April 9

Tomorrow I break the Acme Packing Company case. I have a list of twenty-two Acme employees who we suspect have been stealing meat. Tonight those twenty-two men are still walking around laughing and talking. They don't know they're on this list, and they think nobody knows what they've been doing. By noon tomorrow, after I interrogate them, they won't be laughing anymore.

Acme is the biggest meat-packing plant of its kind in America, with 335 employees. In January it processed and sold fifteen million pounds of meat but failed to earn a dime of profit. Every month there is a big shrinkage. Somebody is stealing meat—tons of it.

The owners called me. I am a private investigator. Who else could they go to? They had no proof that theft was taking place. The FBI won't come in on a case unless there's proof that at least $5,000 is involved and that state lines have been crossed. The police won't come in until you have hard evidence. The client had to come to somebody like me, or he'd soon be bankrupt.

I have had agents in Chicago working on this case for two months. They have collected what little evidence we have—it's not much. It's not enough to get the police to do anything, much less the FBI. We have evidence against only four of the twenty-two men.

But the rest are probably in on it, and probably plenty more as well. Of the 335 employees, the owners say there are only five that they are sure are *not* stealing.

I came to Chicago accompanied by John Stano and John Coleman, who are the principal agents working on this case, and by two associates, each of whom brought a portable polygraph machine—what people call a lie detector.

I figure I have about three minutes to make each suspect confess. If he won't confess, we have to let him go. We don't have enough evidence to do anything else. If he won't sign a confession, the owners can't even fire him, because of union protection of employees. The thieves will go right on working here and will probably go right on stealing. And without a lot of confessions proving how big this ring is and how successfully it has operated over a long period of time, the owners can't recover a cent from the bonding company.

The owners will also be out the $15,000 to $18,000 they've already paid us, and to top it off the thieves might even get together with a smart lawyer and start a suit.

A lot rides on these interrogations. I am an expert at extracting confessions. That's what I do. The owners just told me that there was at least $100,000 insurance money riding on my interrogations. Did I think I could get confessions?

We would find that out very quickly. If I do my job right, we are going to get confessions. I will ask the thieves to confess and they will do it. The nature of guilt is such that they have no choice. Guilt is something that everyone in this world feels.

Everyone. I don't care how tough or amoral a person considers himself, he feels guilt pangs from time to time. A murderer feels guilt when he thinks the police are closing in. My wife feels guilt when she's not sure whether there's enough money in her account to cover the check she is writing.

Everybody is guilty of something, and if this guilt involves criminal acts, it keeps building up. The guilty person is constantly thinking, "When are they going to catch up to me?"

Guilt is both mental and physical. A man's body reacts to his degree of guilt. Some years ago in Alabama I interrogated a man who had been stealing from the auto parts store where he worked. My agents had actually seen him put money in his pocket. The interrogation took place in my hotel room. In those days it took me longer to break a suspect than it does now. Twenty-five years ago it took me an hour per suspect; ten years ago it took me fifteen minutes. Today I can do it in three minutes or under.

Anyway, I began to work on this suspect. There was no odor in the room when he came in. After about ten minutes the odor was so strong I had to open the window. It was something like the odor of skunk. It got so strong I couldn't stand it. His perspiration glands were telling me he was guilty. If I'd known in advance, I'd have been wearing a gas mask.

I've often been conscious of that odor during an interrogation. Often I've known instantly that a suspect was guilty. I can't tell you how I knew; I sensed it.

I could write a book on guilt alone. Guilt is something that feeds on the future: what will happen to me when caught, what will my defense be? The original criminal act is like the seed of a tree. The tree itself is the future which the guilty man fears.

The guilty person can forget his guilt from time to time, but it keeps coming back to him. The more time that passes, the more criminal acts he commits, the more guilt he feels. It becomes for the suspect like a crystal glass which fills up with the money he steals, all of it in coins. As time passes that glass gets bigger and bigger, more and more full, and more and more fragile. Then I come in, and I give that glass a tap. If I tap it right, it will shatter, and all those coins will spill out on the floor. The suspect will then sign a confession and be relieved at the chance to do so.

This is the theory, if everything goes right. But a lot could go wrong tomorrow.

We are here in the Holiday Inn on North Marine Drive. Getting the luggage out of the taxi, I conked my head on the trunk lid. It bled a little and it throbs and I'm holding ice on it as I dictate this. I am 65 years old and have been doing this job for thirty-six years.

The client and his associates have come to see me. They are very nervous and want to know exactly what I am going to do. What is my procedure; how do I expect to get confessions? I promise nothing. I tell them the truth, that there are a lot of things about this setup I don't like. I wouldn't be surprised if we get nothing at all tomorrow.

The case is this: In April, 1970, a little over a year ago, the client, Mr. Straus, called me. His profits were way down, maybe there was some theft going on in his meat-packing plant. He asked me for help.

I recommended that we assign a black agent to this plant because many of the employees were black. The area where this agent was assigned had a couple of hundred employees, and ordinarily in a situation like that a man would require several weeks to develop friendships, particularly if the plant is located in a big city like Chicago. A man's got to blend in with other employees, to gain their confidence, and they've got to feel he's one of their own. But after my agent, a man named Vincent, had been at the plant for six weeks, the client decided that nothing earthshaking was developing. So he decided not to continue our services.

At this point it had cost him around $1,500. Mr. Straus was paying Agent Vincent a regular meat packer's salary; in addition, he paid us a fee of about $250 a week to develop the information. At that point the client decided that perhaps he'd made a mistake in his figures. Shrinkage may have been bad. In his own mind he rationalized that there was nothing big going on. Now he felt that maybe people were taking a few cuts of beef or pork loins, whereas previously he had thought that people were walking out with whole quarters of beef.

Almost a year went by before one of his employees came to a top executive of the company and told him that there was wholesale stealing going on. The informant, a man named Hubert Tinsley, came to Tony Vitale, an ex-truck driver who had become general manager, and told him that he'd spotted an Acme trailer backed up to the Eisman Supermarket and that some merchandise was being unloaded. When Tony Vitale checked his records, he found that their plant didn't sell to Eisman. So Mr. Straus called us again and asked us to make another investigation.

Before we started this second investigation, I sent one of my associates to Chicago from our home office to talk to the informant, Tinsley, and get specific details. Usually when an informant comes to the owners, he talks in generalities. The owners don't know how to get specific information or how to ask the right questions. They get so excited when someone tells them they're being robbed that they forget about facts and details. All they know is that employees are robbing them.

My associate met with Mr. Vitale and with Hubert Tinsley, who mentioned seven people who he felt sure were involved and some others that he only thought were involved. The only specific thing he was able to report was that on one occasion he saw an Acme trailer backed up to the Eisman Supermarket at 3769 South Wisconsin Avenue.

After a conference in our home office, we decided that we

should take the job, and the first thing we did was to send an agent to Chicago to watch this supermarket. He spent two weeks watching from a parked car, and absolutely nothing happened. Nothing at all. It's possible that when the agent left to go to the bathroom or to get something to eat he could have missed the action.

The FBI or the police department can afford to have five cars tailing any subject and running down parallel streets, or parked twenty-four hours a day outside a shop. A private investigator, where the client is paying the bill, has got to watch his expenses. You can't recommend having two, four, five agents staked outside one store. It would cost the client more than he was losing. At this point, however, the client stated that he desperately wanted this information, so we took the luxury of sending two agents to cover the store. On the second day with two agents watching, we caught a delivery of merchandise. Our agent, John Stano, saw an Acme truck driver take a 180-pound side of beef from truck number 28 into the store. The truck backed up to the delivery entrance. There were two men in it, one white and one black. The white male driver got out and opened the back door. Agent Stano described him as 6'1", 190 pounds, long sideburns, a beard, about 27 years old. He took one side of meat inside the store. The other man, black, heavyset, around 30 years old, wearing a white hard hat and sunglasses, did not get out. The license number of the truck was 2003-R, and the number on the side of the truck was 28. Later on, when we checked with Acme officials, we discovered that the driver of the truck was named Joe Shopovic. Agents Stano and Coleman watched the store all week, and nothing more happened. The following Tuesday, something did. At about 2:13 P.M. an Acme Packing Company truck came in, number 28, license number 2003-R. The driver got out first. He was white, 6'2", 180 pounds, about 27 years old, and was wearing a Fu Man Chu type beard. He had brown hair and long sideburns—Shopovic. The other man then got out of the truck. He was white, 5'10", 160 pounds, about 22 years old, and was wearing a black wool head cover. The driver then carried one side of meat into the store and the helper followed behind. The helper was later identified as Mario Alonghi.

Agent Stano was staked out from February 25 to March 21. He spent the first two weeks sitting alone behind the store looking for the Acme truck. He sat there from nine o'clock in the morning until nine o'clock at night. He talked to himself, read, wrote letters, listened to the radio. It was cold. He turned the engine on and off to keep the car heated. We had assumed there was a pattern, and he was hoping to find out what that pattern was. But nothing happened.

Stano was worried about being spotted. The first week he parked in the lot behind the unloading dock. He changed cars every day. He used rented cars, and at night he would drive them out to the airport and exchange them. He'd come back to the lot the next morning driving a different make and a different model. And he'd park in a different part of the lot. No one ever came out onto the dock to see if the place was under surveillance.

For twelve hours a day Stano watched that store. After the second week, we sent another agent so they could at least switch off from time to time. We had two cars, one agent in each.

During the third week, Stano parked out on the street. Those Acme trailer trucks were easy to spot. When he finally spotted one, he drove into the lot and parked close enough to get the license number and a general description of the man going into the store and of what he was carrying.

While we were watching the store, we had also decided to follow some trucks. Mr. Vitale, although I had warned him about arousing the suspicions of his employees, got the itinerary of these trucks by asking some questions, which he normally didn't do. The net result was that nothing happened at the Eisman Supermarket after that because the word had gone around that somebody was thinking about doing something— or at least that's what we assumed. Although there was no more activity at that particular store, we picked up activity in others. We followed a black driver by the name of Alvin Johns. Stano saw him deliver meat to an A & P market, and his helper, Roosevelt Taylor, was with him.

Acme handled fifteen million pounds of meat in January without showing a profit. They were petrified, panicked. On February 19, they finally saw their records for January. Their markup on meat is only 3 percent, and their profit is 1 percent. The illegal meat that we picked up leaving their plant was peanuts compared to what they had been losing in other ways.

We had other agents search through records at the courthouse and watch the houses where these suspects live. One week we had six agents in Chicago working on the background to the case. We found out that Alvin Johns had once been convicted of aggravated battery. He received two years probation which ended on November 12, 1965. We also found out that Shopovic had been arraigned on three counts stemming from an attempted arson of a Jewish community center. Shopovic was 28 at the time and was found not guilty on all three counts. An alibi from a friend was his primary defense.

When Agent Stano actually saw one crooked transaction at Eisman's, confirming for the first time the information of the informant, Hubert Tinsley, Acme management ordered me to go all out. More than $100,000 had been stolen. They didn't even know how that much meat could be gotten out of the plant.

When we discovered that stolen meat was being taken into the Eisman Supermarket, we wanted to be sure that we could protect our case. If we didn't get any more information, we intended to bolster our position by having one of our own agents buy wholesale meat at the regular price and then try to sell it illegally to this crooked butcher. The butcher would think he was buying stolen meat. This would have three effects: (1) it would establish beyond question that stolen merchandise was being bought and sold there; (2) the butcher would believe my agent a thief like himself and so might reveal information to him; and (3) I would be able to lean on this butcher later, if necessary, to make him give evidence against the Acme drivers.

Agent John Coleman was sent out to buy pork, not from Acme, but from other packers, for we didn't want to risk exposing the identity of our client. The first sale was some pork round. Agent Coleman went into the store to see the butcher, Chris. Chris said he had been buying meat at less than 33 cents a pound. He took Coleman to Eisman, the owner, a man about 32 years old. Eisman asked him whether the meat was hot. Coleman told him it was, and Eisman said he didn't want to fool with it.

They stood there in the grocery aisles. Coleman said, "There's no point in my lying to you, the meat is definitely hot. That's the way I'm trying to make my profit," but Eisman still insisted that he didn't want the hot meat. Coleman made as if to walk out.

Then Eisman looked at Coleman and said, "Well, I can't trust you."

"Well, I can't trust you either—you could have the cops on me before I get out of here."

"Well, I wouldn't do that."

"I can't trust you any more than you can trust me."

"Your deal sounds interesting, although I am afraid to take the risk."

Coleman said, "Well, no use my wasting your time."

"Well, wait a minute." Eisman looked at Chris behind the meat counter. Chris nodded his head that he believed Coleman was all right. So Eisman said, "OK, so I'm going to trust you. Bring me what you've got."

The first deal was for seventy-two pounds of pork round.

Eisman said, "Do you have it with you now?"

"No."

"You do not have it now?"

"I do not have it now."

Coleman made a mistake by not having the meat with him. When he came back with the meat, Eisman should have been afraid of a setup. Coleman could have had the cops waiting. But that's where greed gets them all. Greed is the motivating factor in the whole operation, and Eisman had the deal. Because of that greed to make that extra money, Eisman let his guard down and said, "OK. What time can you be back?"

"Well, somewhere around noon." Coleman left him and went for the meat.

Coleman had already been on surveillance for a couple of weeks behind the place and knew every inch of it, but he parked the car away from the delivery entrance.

"Well," Eisman said when Coleman came back, "where are you parked?"

"On the street."

Eisman said, "Well, bring it to the back."

"Well, how do I know where the back is?"

"Well, come on, I'll show you."

Coleman had a car with the meat in the trunk. Eisman wanted to see the automobile registration. Coleman told him he couldn't show any papers on it. It was his uncle's.

Eisman asked, "It's your uncle's car, a brand new car like this?"

"The meat is hot and you stand there talking to me? I'm trying to deal with you and I'm hoping you'll deal with me and if my uncle knew I was hauling hot meat in his car, he'd be ready to skin me."

"OK. Bring the meat on in." Coleman threw it up on the dock. They made the deal.

Coleman paid $43 for the pork and sold it for $20. Eisman would have had to pay $43 wholesale. He's doing all this for $23. For $23 he's becoming a criminal. But he's doing it over and over again.

Coleman went back there nine times. Once we decided it was safe to move in with Acme merchandise, Coleman was able to question Eisman in a casual way. Coleman learned that Eisman was dealing with someone else at Acme, but no name was given. Eisman said he had never paid more than 33 cents a pound for meat before. This entire matter was overheard by Chris, the butcher. Coleman sold Eisman loins, ribs, and bacon. He was told that if be brought beef, he would get $35 for every $90 hind shank. Eisman mentioned he had been in this racket for seven years.

Coleman learned that Eisman was married, resided at 9133 Hazel Avenue in Niles, and supposedly had two girlfriends. We began to do surveillance on Eisman's home, a two-story duplex, white brick with light blue trimming, in a middle-income neighborhood. He drove a 1966 Buick. A Dun & Bradstreet report on Eisman showed $15,000 cash, $70,000 merchandise, $30,000 fixed assets, $15,000 accounts payable and bank notes of $73,800. We were not hired to catch Eisman although he was more crooked than the truck drivers he bought from.

Our whole case boiled down to the evidence we had against Shopovic, Alonghi, Johns, and Taylor. Our man, Agent Stano, saw Shopovic deliver meat to Eisman on two occasions. Mario Alonghi was the helper on Shopovic's truck the second time. We were unable to determine who the helper was the first time. Agent Stano saw Alvin Johns, a second driver, deliver meat to two other supermarkets. Roosevelt Taylor was the lugger and helper on Johns' truck for both deliveries. Those are the four prime suspects. All we saw were those few occasions when meat was delivered. In other words, all four men at the interrogation tomorrow morning could just deny the fact that we ever saw them. We have never even been able to make a purchase from them. If they're smart, all they'll say is: "Go to hell, you son of a bitch. I never delivered meat, I don't even know where the place is—never heard of the goddamn place. Who in the hell do you think you're kidding? Go to hell and forget the whole goddamn thing." If they're smart that's exactly what they'd say.

Now, if they say that, and we're blown out of the tub right then, we might as well discontinue the interrogation, because if we stir up any more people, and all of them get together and start thinking, we could damn well have a lawsuit on our hands. It's vitally important to get these people to admit their involvement right off. Tomorrow I've got three to four minutes with each subject, and if I don't succeed then, it's all over. We lose.

Now then, if that happens all we have left is our insurance, Mr. Eisman. I show him Agent Coleman, who he thinks he bought stolen meat from. I will let him believe Coleman has been caught and arrested, and I'll offer him a deal. He's a businessman. Eisman might be made to pinpoint the various people that he bought meat from. If he wants to turn State's Evidence, we can then go to the courts and have these drivers arrested. Eisman would be the prime witness against them. Eisman also could tell me to go to hell, but the chances, I think, are less. If I have John Coleman in the car and tell Eisman I want him to come out and see our evidence against him, and I show him John—I don't know what he could do but talk. And if I have to, I can tell him I could get the IRS interested in him and that a lot of other things are involved. I could say, "I can't promise you a damn thing, but you've got a fifty-fifty chance if you turn State's Evidence." Eisman runs around with women. He's a married man. We know a lot about him. At the proper time those innuendoes can be thrown at him, and they might be very helpful.

If it comes to this, Eisman might accuse me of blackmail, and some liberals might agree with him. My answer would be that I'm not playing with children—I'm playing with people who steal merchandise. Someone like Eisman can't tell me what's just and what's equitable. What the hell is justice in this case? I don't intend to threaten Eisman, but if the only way to solve this case is to fight fire with fire, I will do it.

But even with Eisman as insurance, we don't have much of a case. The client thinks there is a ring operating in his plant, because stealing on such a big scale has to involve not only the stickmen and the drivers, but the scalers and some of the clerical help as well. We don't know who any of these people might be. At one time all the paperwork relating to a particular shipment that was suspect disappeared. There has to be collusion.

We don't know who's in this and who's not. The general manager, Tony Vitale, has been the man in the middle. He has not been the most cooperative person. As a former truck driver, his sympathy is more with his men. He's still a union member, even though he is now management.

The four names at the top of my list should lead—they must lead—to others who are not on my list at all. The client wants to empty that place out tomorrow, to fire everybody who's been stealing.

The first few minutes are going to tell the story for the whole day, and these first four men are not easy subjects. They're big, they're tough. My men have sat surveillance on them. We've watched them pick up 150 pounds of meat with one hand, throw it over their shoulders, and walk in with it and in a second be back to grab another one. These guys can stand flatfooted in a cooler with one of these big meathooks, and without moving the lower part of their bodies at all, just by using their shoulders, they can lift a 150-pound piece of meat and roll it down that roller just with their arm power, 140, 150 pounds.

Two of the four men have been arrested before. When you're

talking to an individual who's been arrested and been exposed to the courts, who knows he beat a rap before, he's not likely to respond to anything I tell him. It isn't as if you were going to upset their family life, give their wives the shock of finding out they're not angels, or their neighbors finding out something bad about them. These men don't give a damn one way or the other. They're really tough people.

If we crack this case, it will be a miracle. We didn't get any investigative breaks because the clients messed the program up when they started getting information from the men within the plant and aroused their suspicions.

It was information we had to have—itineraries of the trucks —and which stops were scheduled so as to know which were the illegal ones.

After the client began trying to get information on the itineraries from the drivers, the drivers started bringing meat back, saying that their truck was overloaded. They were trying to show that they were honest by bringing meat back.

The men who were overloading the trucks might not have got the information which the drivers had; namely, that the heat was on. So the guys inside the plant were still overloading the trucks. It was too late to interrupt the overloading process, but the drivers were protecting themselves.

Tomorrow morning I'll take Shopovic on at eight o'clock. If I come out smiling at five after eight, that means we've got 'em. If I don't come out for a long time, that's bad. The longer an interrogator talks, the weaker he gets and the stronger the subject gets. We've seen that in every interrogation. If the guy is smart, he would say, "Have me arrested, go ahead. I am ready to go, have me arrested."

If you don't move to arrest him, he knows you don't have a damn thing. Forget it.

Of course, not all subjects confess. The less education a man has, the more hardened a criminal he is, and the older he is, the less chance there is he will confess.

With luck, Shopovic will confess and will also implicate others. I don't know what I will say to him to make him confess. I really don't. I don't know what he looks like; I can't see his Adam's apple moving yet. I can't see him in the second that I am going to bust into him.

I can accuse him, demand a confession, and get it, all in probably a minute or a minute and a half of actual speaking.

How am I going to approach him? I've got to make that decision based on what he looks like. If I say the wrong thing at first inadvertently, the wrong thing, I am dead.

I will look at him with my eyes half closed, with a cigar in my mouth, looking as if I know more than I do; and then I am going to bust into him.

I've heard that some of the so-called master interrogators of my time say you have to lead up to the subject of stealing slowly. I think they are wrong. Three minutes is all it takes. You don't have to know everything that can possibly be known about the subject. You get in there, size him up, and go for his throat. You will have your confession in three minutes.

That's the theory. But this whole goddamn thing tomorrow could go right through the drain.

It happens.

What chapter will that be?

You are dealing with personality, you are dealing with individuals. You just can't predict what any individual is going to do at any given time. I may get him at the wrong time. Maybe the following day or an hour later I could have broken him quickly. He may not be in the right mood. I may have picked the wrong individual to interrogate first.

This is a big day for everybody. The client is liable to get $100,000 from his insurance company, and Coleman and Stano are liable to get $500 bonuses. But I may not get anywhere with Shopovic. He won't be a pushover. He admits things and then always explains them. The client says that Shopovic will give me a fast admission and then a bullshit explanation. Suppose Shopovic tells me: "Sure I took some beef over to Eisman's. So-and-so in the plant put it on the truck and said it was a special the boss wanted delivered that day." He *could* say that—if he thinks of it. These guys think of some pretty fancy answers. But I'll cut him off and say, "Not acceptable."

As I told Mr. Vitale, when he calls that first guy in to be interrogated, I want him to leave the plant floor without too many people knowing about it. After I've been there for an hour and have talked to two or three subjects, there will be a helluva lot of people in the plant who will be aware that something is going on. They will start building up their defenses, and we will have lost the element of surprise. When that fourth or fifth man comes in, he is going to be tough. We have nothing on him or a very weak case, so the chances of our getting an admission from him are very remote. He'll know there's something cooking and will be prepared.

Surprise is 90 percent of any success I will have. Alvin Johns and Roosevelt Taylor, whom I will take after Shopovic, are black. Ten years ago blacks were tough. Today there is no difference between blacks and whites. Ten years ago the black man didn't have his pride involved. No matter who came to see them, they didn't know anything, they had a blank expression, and they wouldn't talk. Now they want to justify themselves. I can tell a black man: "You ought to know better than that. You are the guy who needs to set an example for everybody." Sometimes that statement is enough to make him admit his guilt. I can break a black man easily today. Sometimes they are easier today than the white man.

One of the owners of the Acme Meat Packing Company, who is 74 years old, wants to come to the office tomorrow. It's his day to come in, but I don't want him there. He hasn't previously been told about the thefts, and suddenly he learns that someone is ruining his business. Five minutes after he gets there everyone in the plant will know there's an interrogation going on. Men will start rigging alibis before I even see them.

The amount of money that industry is losing these days is unbelievable. When they start quoting $3 billion or $5 billion a year, that is merely a drop in the bucket. Here we have just one case: our client sold fifteen million pounds of beef in one month and didn't make a dime. You mean to tell me $3 billion or $5 billion a year nationwide is realistic? I'd say that if we have ten employees in any given location, at least five of them are stealing; and of that five, two or three of them are taking the company for plenty. The others are just nickel-and-dime men.

The companies are only interested in making sales, but if they stopped thinking of sales and tried to control what is being stolen, what's going out the back door, they would be making more money. They could make fewer sales and still make more money, but they are not watching the back door. They are not even listening to their accountants. The accountant comes in with figures that show only a small profit this month, when in fact the profit should have been double that. The fact that the company made a profit is satisfactory. They don't stop to think of how much they lost to thefts. Acme sold fifteen million pounds of meat in January. How much profit should they have made? Their normal profit rate is about 1 percent. If fifteen million pounds sell for 50 cents a pound, that's $7.5 million. One percent of that is $75,000 a month, which means that the company is losing nearly a million dollars a year in profit. That's why they spend the time and effort with us. They're talking about a million bucks.

These thefts have probably been going on for years, but the employees have most likely been stealing less than they did in January. It may sound as if that one month is what did them in as crooks, because the management finally got alarmed. But in fact management didn't really get alarmed until the informant, Hubert Tinsley, blew the whistle. It was at this point that they decided to look at their figures. They then saw that they didn't make any money in January.

At the start of tomorrow's interrogation, or any interrogation, I will be in the room alone with the suspect. It is much easier for someone to admit stealing in front of one person than in front of two or more—and there will be no tape recorder. I bust into him, he cracks, and then he agrees to sign a confession. After I get the admission, I bring in the client. Once the client comes in, the subject has known him for years and he is going to start alibiing immediately. I want to get him sewed up first before the client comes in. Sometimes you find clients that are just scared to death and feel sorry for their employees. They are often nervous as hell, but the minute that one guy admits it, they become the biggest shot in the world. They start getting tough with these guys. They were like little lambs before and then they get tough.

Tomorrow, about 7:30 A.M., I start with Shopovic. I've never seen him; he's never seen me.

Anybody who admits anything is insane. They can tell me to go to hell and they should. Maybe they will. If Shopovic refuses to talk, if the No. 2 guy also walks out on me, then my whole deal just went right down the rat hole.

April 10
6 A.M.

I've been up half an hour already studying my notes.

The story of this informant, Hubert Tinsley, doesn't ring true. There's something wrong with it. He's 57 years old and looking for a better job, an inside job. At one point he decided to play detective, too, and he took some meat around to a National

Foods Store and sold it at half price as stolen meat. They told him they would buy all he could get. How did Hubert Tinsley know to go to that store?

There's something fishy about his whole story—not enough specific information, perhaps. Not a single detail about who the other men in the ring are or how they're getting the meat out.

I've decided to interrogate Hubert Tinsley, our own informant, first.

7:30 A.M.

I have just looked over the plant layout. It's not good. The plant is about a hundred yards square and one story high, with a row of offices along one side. The rest is what they call the cooler—an enormous refrigerator about the size of a football field, full of meat hanging from hooks, meat piled on tables. There are 250 butchers in there chopping meat, and the temperature is 38 degrees. In the office section there are only two private offices. The rest are open glass cubicles. A number of the offices, including the two private ones, have a heavy refrigerator door going through into the cooler. These doors open and shut every few minutes, with people in bloody smocks going in and out of the cooler.

We have only the two private offices to use for interrogation. I have ordered the doors to the cooler locked. Supposedly, no one in the glass cubicles knows who we are or why we are here. No one working in the cooler knows we are here yet.

I have also been shown an employees' club room upstairs over the garage. There are mechanics in the garage below working on trucks. They will, of course, see any pedestrian traffic going to or from this club room and will start rumors at once.

7:45 A.M.

I just told one of the clients, Carl Schroeder, that I wanted to take Hubert Tinsley, the informant, first. He called over Tony Vitale. They both assured me that Tinsley was a good man, that there was no possibility he would double-cross us, or that he was a double agent. He couldn't possibly be in on the stealing. What could I do? You have to go along with the client. I told them to send in Shopovic.

8:05 A.M.

Vitale brought Shopovic in. Mr. Vitale said no more than what I had told him to say: "This is Mr. Lipman. He'd like to talk to you."

Shopovic is a big tough-looking guy. He wears a beard and a shirt cut off at the top of the sleeves. He has tattoos on his arms.

I asked his age, address, marital status, and so forth. I was friendly. I gave him a big smile. He thought I was doing a survey of some kind, I suppose. Then, the big contrast, I told him that I was a private investigator, that he was stealing company meat, and that I could prove it. He didn't change the expression on his face. He started denying it.

He wouldn't break. He just kept lying to me. He never heard of the Eisman Supermarket, and he didn't know anyone named Eisman to whom he had sold stolen meat.

I called my agent, Stano, in from the next room: "Is this the man you saw carry meat into Eisman's on March 9 and again on March 16?"

"Yes, sir."

This didn't faze Joe Shopovic one bit. He wasn't the man Stano had seen. He wouldn't do such a thing. I told Shopovic I knew about his police record. He said that he wasn't guilty of bombing that synagogue either and that he had beaten the rap. He had never admitted his guilt even though he said the police had beaten him up badly.

I called in Carl Schroeder and Tony Vitale. Shopovic went right on lying. He wouldn't admit a thing.

I have sent him over to the club room with Stano. We have to keep him out of sight if we are to have any chance with the other twenty-one names on my list. It will be uphill from here on. Shopovic was my key.

I'll take Mario Alonghi next. He was the helper on Shopovic's truck on the second delivery to Eisman. That's all we've got on him.

There are only four names on this list against whom we have anything at all, and I've just used one of them up. After asking Alonghi his name, age, marital status, and so forth, I'm going to accuse Alonghi of months of stealing, based on one delivery as a helper, and hope that the abrupt contrast, the surprise, the shock of being accused will make him confess his own involvement and begin to name the rest of the ring. After that I've got to make him tell how the ring operates. And we've got nothing on him. He may be innocent. The whole thing is crazy.

(Editor's note: It was now 8:08 A.M. Alonghi appeared in the corridor following Mr. Schroeder. Alonghi, who was wearing a bloody butcher smock, was a chunky young man with a round face and long sideburns. He was starting to grow a mustache. He looked confident enough. He had no idea he was about to be accused of stealing. He went into the office with Mr. Lipman, and the door was closed. For the next five minutes, Carl Schroeder stared at that closed door. In the corridor no one spoke. Then the door opened to reveal Mr. Lipman chewing on a dead cigar. Alonghi sat slumped in a chair. There was no more confidence left in him. He had cracked, and presently his defeat would

make him surly. It was 8:12 A.M. What follows is the transcript of the tape which began turning at this time.)

LIPMAN: Is Mr. Carl Schroeder out there? Will you come in here please, Carl? Mario Alonghi here is trying to level with us, Carl. It's just that he can't think of everything that's been going on around here all at once. He's 22 years old and married with two kids. He was in the army and worked here before 1967 and came back on April 28, 1970. For the past ten months this stealing has been going on, as far as he knows. He knows there is another man in the plant involved. Is that right, Mario? Right now Mario is trying to remember how they get the meat out of here. He'd like to tell us about it, if he can remember. Is that right, Mario? Now Mario can't remember if he's ever been out with Joe Shopovic, even though we saw that transaction, but he did go out as helper on a truck with a driver by the name of Augie DeFelice, and they sold some stolen meat. The first time around, DeFelice gave him about $70; this was before Christmas. The next time he gave him $20, and the third time, $15. After DeFelice gave the $70 he realized that Mario was okay, and then he started cutting down on him, explaining that he had to cut somebody else in on the deal. The first time, the $70 operation, DeFelice said he screwed some guy out of his cut. Is that right, Mario?

ALONGHI: He must have cut somebody.

LIPMAN: Mario has also been out with Alvin Johns, the driver. Mario got $20 or $25 on a delivery of stolen meat that Johns made, right? These three deals with Augie DeFelice—were they all made to the Eisman Supermarket, Mario?

ALONGHI: Yes.

LIPMAN: Was all that merchandise, all that beef, put on the truck in the same manner?

ALONGHI: All loaded up the same way.

LIPMAN: Can you tell me for my own satisfaction, because I have never worked in a packing plant, I don't know anything about a packing plant . . .

ALONGHI: You're not missing much.

LIPMAN: So tell me how you think that merchandise gets on the truck.

ALONGHI: They are out there moving that pin.

LIPMAN: What pin? I don't even know what a pin is.

ALONGHI: Well, the hind quarters are hanging from hooks, and the hooks slide along a rail. When he brings five pieces up to the scale, he's got the pin on the last piece, and those five are weighed in full and are pushed onto the truck. How hard would it be to push six pieces across and move the pin up? That must be how it's done, it's common sense. That's the only way meat could be put on without somebody catching you.

LIPMAN: I want you to recall when DeFelice was operating that truck. Try to remember who was loading that truck, who was pushing that beef that day.

ALONGHI: You are there all day long, five days a week, day after day. You never know who is pushing that stuff on. You don't pay no attention to it. You're busy, you're working.

LIPMAN: Who are the guys who would be pushing it on? There are only two or three guys who could be pushing it on, right?

ALONGHI: Midnight Shadow, James Jackson, and Butch.

LIPMAN: Midnight Shadow? Who is Midnight Shadow?

ALONGHI: I don't know what his real name is. He works five days a week.

LIPMAN: Is it Roosevelt Taylor? What did you say his name is? Midnight Shadow?

ALONGHI: That's what we call him. He's a colored man, and the white guys call him Midnight Shadow.

LIPMAN: You mentioned three guys: Roosevelt Taylor, and James Jackson are the first two. Who is the other guy?

ALONGHI: The only other one would be Butch, and I don't think he had anything to do with it.

LIPMAN: Butch?

ALONGHI: That's what we call him—Butch.

LIPMAN: What's his name?

ALONGHI: I don't know his name.

LIPMAN: Is he white?

ALONGHI: No, he's colored.

LIPMAN: Is Roosevelt Taylor colored?

ALONGHI: Yes.

LIPMAN: James Jackson, is he colored?

ALONGHI: Yes.

LIPMAN: Assuming you don't know who is involved, could you take a wild guess as to which one seems to be the man?

ALONGHI: Well, they are the men who are pushing the meat onto the scale. There are only two or three guys doing it.

LIPMAN: You just mentioned the three of them. If you had a choice of the man, who would it be?

ALONGHI: I wouldn't blame anybody.

LIPMAN: You said that Butch you didn't think was involved, that leaves it to two.

ALONGHI: I don't know. I said I think, but I don't know for sure, or positively.

LIPMAN: You mean you've never discussed it in the truck or talked about it?

ALONGHI: They don't talk about whoever is connected with it. I've never been told. When I come in here at night and get out of the truck, I punch out and go home. If the men talk about it later on, during the next day or the next night, I don't know about it.

LIPMAN: They slip you something because you're a helper, just to keep you quiet?

ALONGHI: Yes, that's right. Naturally, I'm getting something.

LIPMAN: These guys, Midnight Shadow and James Jackson, they don't know who is going to be driving the truck that they are pushing the extra meat onto?

ALONGHI: Well, usually they do, and even if the meat comes back, then it comes back.

LIPMAN: How often does it come back. Not often, huh?

ALONGHI: No.

SCHROEDER: Every single driver is involved?

ALONGHI: I wouldn't say every single driver. The stickmen know who they can trust. They know who is taking an extra load because if there is a truck out there being loaded, the scaler knows who is getting the truck, so naturally they know from the scaler.

SCHROEDER: Listen, this is so big that everybody here is involved. Is that what you're saying?

ALONGHI: Like I said, I've been with the three drivers and that's all I know, and I'll take a lie detector test and anything else, 'cause I am not lying. I want to save my ass, too.

LIPMAN: We feel you are intelligent enough to know who you are getting involved with, that you would have to know for your own self-satisfaction and protection. Then if anything happens, you not only know the driver, you know the man on the inside, too. That's only self-preservation.

ALONGHI: Now you are putting me down. You think I am lying, and I am not.

LIPMAN: I want you to go into the next room. We want to straighten out the one transaction.

ALONGHI: I am not going to do it.

LIPMAN: You will not do it?

ALONGHI: Why should I? I am going to lose my job, and everybody in the plant is going to know I am a fink. That don't make no sense. It don't. I might as well go out and holler in the plant that I'm finking. It's stupid.

LIPMAN: Stealing is bad, isn't it?

ALONGHI: Right, but why should I have to be the patsy, the fall guy, the fink?

SCHROEDER: How do you know somebody hasn't talked about you?

ALONGHI: Maybe they have. Maybe you have it all in black and white.

LIPMAN: How did I get it? I didn't get it though the air, did I?

ALONGHI: I don't know how you got it.

LIPMAN: Well, I don't have a radio with waves going through here to put the bite on you, do I?

ALONGHI: No, no.

LIPMAN: But I got it, right?

ALONGHI: Like I said, I had to go along with selling meat because I was there. What was I going to do, say, "No, no, no, don't do it. I'm here." The guy is going to say, "Take it."

LIPMAN: Why didn't you tell him, "No. You do it, it's your business. Don't give me any business."

ALONGHI: You think anybody is stupid enough to refuse $75 when a guy hands it to you? You know, to a guy like me, who only clears $70 a week, $75 is a lot of money.

LIPMAN: How much are you making a week here?

ALONGHI: Now? $100 to $125 if I am lucky.

LIPMAN: How much do you get paid an hour?

ALONGHI: $1.75

LIPMAN: Do you work forty hours a week?

ALONGHI: Sometimes. Things are slow right now.

LIPMAN: Things are slow because you've been stealing from the company.

ALONGHI: I haven't been. Now you are blaming me.

LIPMAN: Well, you said you were.

ALONGHI: I was just there. I had to be there.

LIPMAN: When you take money, you are just as bad off as the other. You know that. You were a victim of circumstances, but you took advantage of them. You could have gone to the company immediately and told them what the deal was.

ALONGHI: Yeah, right, I could have. I could have. Too many guys work in this plant, and everybody would know about it. I am not going to play the company fink. Nobody would. Nobody, not a single one.

LIPMAN: You want to talk to Shopovic for me?

ALONGHI: Why? Then he will go back and tell the guys I'm the one.

LIPMAN: Let me explain something to you. If one guy, just one guy, doesn't cooperate and everybody else does, that one guy is going to screw it up for everybody; and we are going to have to go a different route. But if everybody does the right thing and cooperates, then nobody is going to get hurt.

ALONGHI: Nobody is going to get hurt, huh? When it gets out that I'm the guy who sat here talking to you, the fall guy, you think I won't get hurt? You already know more than I do, so why am I sitting here?

LIPMAN: You are sitting here because you are involved. That's why you're sitting here.

ALONGHI: I'm sitting here because I am getting blamed.

LIPMAN: No, you are not getting blamed, you are just a victim of circumstances.

ALONGHI: Any man, I don't care who it is, $75 is a lot of money, that meat weighs 150 to 200 pounds. Man, you just don't turn down $75. I mean you have to be stupid. Don't tell me no. I know.

SCHROEDER: In other words, you are saying that you deliberately didn't try to find out any more? You didn't listen when the other guys were talking about it?

ALONGHI: What did I want to know for? When the man gave me $75, I said yeah. Now the man told me one other time that somebody else in the plant wanted to be cut in. That's all he said—he didn't tell me who. Somebody else. This is the way it was told to me.

SCHROEDER: All these different drivers are stealing free-lance? They are not working together? They just take what they can get for themselves, in other words?

ALONGHI: I've told you everything I know. I'll take a lie detector test and say the same thing I just told you. I'll just stay right here in this room. I'm telling the truth right now, all that I can remember.

SCHROEDER: If you keep thinking about it, more might come back to you off and on.

LIPMAN: Joe Shopovic is a tough guy. Didn't you hear any threats, not one?

ALONGHI: No. I don't like people threatening me. If somebody threatens to beat me or kill me or something, I just don't like it.

LIPMAN: All right, Mr. Schroeder, Mario has leveled with us. He told us the facts and that he has been invoived. Mario has been involved with Johns with DeFelice and Shopovic and he has gotten about $200, maybe $300—he don't remember if his life depended on it. Am I right or wrong? You could have gotten $200, you could have gotten $300—you don't know, right?—over the whole period of time. So if you got about $300 and it had to be divided three ways, that's about $900. Eisman Supermarket gives $50 for a hind quarter. Is that about half price, Mr. Schroeder, or less than half?

SCHROEDER: About half.

LIPMAN: So you see, Mr. Schroeder, in this operation alone, that's about $1,800 worth of merchandise. Just in this operation alone.

SCHROEDER: Yeah.

LIPMAN: Here's the story. They steal this meat by shoving an extra hind quarter through when they put that pin on it, right? How many does a truck hold, Mario?

ALONGHI: I couldn't say, about twenty a truck. I think the most extra I've seen pull out on one truck was about three. Other times it was one or two. If they are too overweight, then the weigher takes care of it. If you've got an overweight, there's some difference in the bill, and somebody has to take care of it.

LIPMAN: OK, fellows, let's go in the other room. I want to see Alvin Johns.

(Editor's note: After a short wait, the third suspect appeared in the corridor, again following Mr. Schroeder. Johns was a tall, shambling black man. He had his cap in his hand and looked friendly. He had no idea what was about to happen to him. He went into the office in which Mr. Lipman was waiting. The door closed. Again, Mr. Schroeder stared at the closed door while the minutes ticked away one by one. When the door opened and Lipman invited us inside, the formerly smiling black man looked devastated.)

8:28 A.M.

LIPMAN: You've admitted to me you are involved, Alvin, and now I've opened the door and invited Mr. Schroeder in here so you can tell him about it. I've got to get the facts, Alvin. Tell you what I'm gonna do. I'm going to read you a list of men who might be involved with you. You just answer yes or no. James Jackson.

JOHNS: Yes.

LIPMAN: Al Covello.

JOHNS: No.

LIPMAN: Roosevelt Taylor. He's the one they call Midnight Shadow, isn't he?

JOHNS: Yes.

LIPMAN: Did Joe Shopovic split with you?

JOHNS: Yes.

LIPMAN: Say that. That's all I want to hear.

JOHNS: Yes, he did.

LIPMAN: Roosevelt Taylor, alias Midnight Shadow, is not only the driver, but he has also put merchandise on your truck, is that right?

JOHNS: He's not a driver. He put something on my truck once. I don't know if he put anything more on.

LIPMAN: You cut him in on the money.

JOHNS: Yes.

LIPMAN: Because he put the merchandise on?

JOHNS: Yes.

LIPMAN: Did he tell you before you left on the route that you had extra stuff?

JOHNS: Yes.

LIPMAN: How many quarters did you have?

JOHNS: One.

LIPMAN: Did he tell you where to sell it?

JOHNS: No.

LIPMAN: He left that up to you?

JOHNS: Yes.

LIPMAN: When you came back, how much money did you give him?

JOHNS: I forget. Forty-five dollars.

LIPMAN: How much did James Jackson get of the forty-five?

JOHNS: He got twenty bucks.

LIPMAN: When you first came to work here, you were inside, cutting, right? Until you started driving, you had no knowledge of anything going on, is that right?

JOHNS: Yes.

LIPMAN: Who told you that there was stealing going on?

JOHNS: I went out as helper on the truck with Joe Shopovic. He sold a hind.

LIPMAN: Was that the Eisman Supermarket? A big parking lot, drugstore on the corner?

JOHNS: I don't know.

LIPMAN: What did Joe tell you, actually?

JOHNS: He told me I could make some money.

LIPMAN: He gave you $10 dollars?

JOHNS: Yes.

LIPMAN: What other conversations did you have?

JOHNS: We didn't have no other conversations.

LIPMAN: Did Joe discuss how often he had been doing it? Did he discuss anything about the operation?

JOHNS: No, he did not.

LIPMAN: Did you ever discuss anything afterwards?

JOHNS: Afterwards, he told me I could make money.

LIPMAN: Why don't you step into this other room for a minute?

JOHNS: I didn't lie to you. I told you everything. I worked at another place ten years—they gave me the keys to the place to lock up at night. I never got in no trouble. I get here and I listen to these guys.

SCHROEDER: Do you know anything about Covello, the scaler? Did he ever fix the scales for you? I'm asking about the scalers. Did Covello jack the scales up for you or fix them for you? Did anybody else ever fix the scales for you?

JOHNS: No.

LIPMAN: Just step into the other room now. My assistant will dictate a statement and you can sign it. Carl, I'll take that Captain Midnight.

(Editor's note: In the other office, Mario Alonghi had read over his confession and, in the presence of my assistant and the client, had signed it. Alonghi was now sitting on the floor

against the wall in the main salesmen's office. All around him men were selling meat by telephone. Alonghi had been told to sit there, so there he sat. He was trying to appear surly, but every time anyone looked at him, his eyes dropped. Soon Alonghi would be joined against that wall by Alvin Johns. Meanwhile, Midnight Shadow had been brought to the door of Lipman's office. Lipman, smiling, shook hands with him: "How are you? Good to see you." Then the door closed. In a moment would come the big contrast: "You've been stealing meat." When the door opened again, Shadow, a stocky man wearing a hard hat, was sitting there trying to look unconcerned. Lipman said, "Come in, Carl. Midnight Shadow has admitted he was involved." Lipman then continued his interrogation.)

8:45 A.M.

LIPMAN: If you were a gentleman, Shadow, and I hope you are, you would voluntarily tell us everything that's going on in this plant. You're in a key position. You're not only a lugger, you're a stickman, and you're also a helper on the truck.

MIDNIGHT SHADOW: If you get every beef lugger or truck driver or helper that's worked here any length of time, and if they all tell the truth, you wouldn't have nobody left working here. You got to fire the whole crew.

LIPMAN: You mean they're all getting something? How do they get it?

MIDNIGHT SHADOW: The butchers don't cut that many small steaks, and you mostly get shook down before you get out of here at night. But they get out with it.

LIPMAN: You're no dummy; you're a pretty smart fellow.

MIDNIGHT SHADOW: No, I'm not.

LIPMAN: Yes, you are. You're making a flat statement that every lugger out there, every cutter—90 percent of them—is getting something one way or another. Tell me in your own words, without mentioning any names, how they do it.

MIDNIGHT SHADOW: When you see the men going out of the building, you hear them saying to each other, "You better lighten up. Lighten up there, man."

SCHROEDER: You mean they're going out with their pockets full of meat?

MIDNIGHT SHADOW: What do you think, man?

LIPMAN: I think we've established the fact that we've been pretty square with you, right? I'd like to ask you to help us now. There's a helluva lot that we could do for you. I want to go over a list of names. All I want you to say is yes or no. Is that simple?

MIDNIGHT SHADOW: Yeah.

LIPMAN: You want a cigar? I'll give you a good cigar. I'll give you a 65-cent cigar. Here's the list: Joe Shopovic.

MIDNIGHT SHADOW: Not that I know of.

LIPMAN: What would yes mean?

MIDNIGHT SHADOW: You're talking about taking meat, right?

LIPMAN: Mario Alonghi?

MIDNIGHT SHADOW: No, he's not involved.

LIPMAN: Are you going to tell me no to everybody? You were talking about a lot of people who were doing something. Alvin Johns?

MIDNIGHT SHADOW: Well, yes.

LIPMAN: Roosevelt Taylor, known as Captain Midnight?

MIDNIGHT SHADOW: Yes, definitely.

LIPMAN: Al Covello?

MIDNIGHT SHADOW: I've never been out with him.

LIPMAN: Steve Dzerovitch?

MIDNIGHT SHADOW: No.

LIPMAN: You're not trying to help me.

MIDNIGHT SHADOW: I can't tell you what I don't know.

SCHROEDER: Hubert Tinsley?

MIDNIGHT SHADOW: I've never been out with him.

LIPMAN: Sonny Mapes?

MIDNIGHT SHADOW: I've never been out with him.

LIPMAN: Do you want to run down this list again and you tell me what you've heard? Not what you know for sure, but what you've heard?

MIDNIGHT SHADOW: I can't tell what I don't know.

LIPMAN: All these people you haven't heard anything about?

MIDNIGHT SHADOW: Is that all the names you got on your list?

LIPMAN: There's no point in going on.

SCHROEDER: Did somebody organize all this, or did all the individual drivers and stickmen work it out for themselves?

MIDNIGHT SHADOW: To my mind, that's exactly what happened.

SCHROEDER: Somebody has to have organized this thing, and you guys are taking the rap for him.

MIDNIGHT SHADOW: You can only tell what you know. I can only tell you what I did, and that's that.

SCHROEDER: Who's the big man? Is it James Jackson?

LIPMAN: If you'll step next door please, Shadow, my assistant will dictate a statement for you to sign. . . . Carl, I'll take James Jackson next. If this door opens five minutes from now and I'm smiling, you'll know we've broken this case.

(Editor's note: Alonghi, Johns, and Shadow had all signed statements; they sat glumly against the wall in the salesmen's office. Lipman was now closed in with James Jackson, whom he believed to be the ringleader. The door opened once more.)

9:05 A.M.

LIPMAN: James, let's back off a few minutes. I told you it's been going on six months. In fact, this thing started in 1968—it's been three years that you've been involved in it. Let's not kid ourselves about it. I know that, based on what these other people have told me.

I'll tell you how this thing happened, James. One guy needed a little extra dough, and he told you, James Jackson, to just put some extra meat on there. It was very easy for you as the stickman to just push another one over, wasn't it?

This thing has been going on for three years. What have you been doing with all this extra money? You need all the help you can get, James. You're 51 years old. For God's sake, you need all the help you can get. You're raising a family. Do you want these kids raised up knowing that you're in jail? What do you want to do, do you want to work this thing out here, or not?

JACKSON: If there's any way possible.

LIPMAN: All right, then you tell me who you're dealing with— all the drivers whose trucks you've been pushing meat onto.

VITALE: Whose idea was it? Who started the thing? That don't make any difference, really. I'm just curious.

SCHROEDER: Tell me one thing, James. Was Hubert Tinsley in on this with you?

JACKSON: Yes.

(Editor's note: Now the interrogations went faster, and between each one Lipman was smiling broadly. The signed confessions were brought to him and went into his breast pocket.

They brought in a tall, pasty-skinned truck driver named Augie DeFelice. The office door closed. Presently it opened again.)

9:40 A.M.

DEFELICE: I'm only talking because I don't want to get fired. I stole some meat. Everybody was doing it. This is the best job I ever had, and I'm loyal to the company and don't want to lose my job.

LIPMAN: You knew Eisman in the past, did you?

DEFELICE: The first time I went there, we had an extra quarter on the truck, and Steve Dzerovitch said to me, "Do you want to get rid of it?"

I said: "I don't like taking those kind of chances. It's easy for you because you're single. You got shit. I got a fucking car, I got a wife who's not working."

He said: "Well, let's try it." It worked out.

LIPMAN: How did you know it was James Jackson putting it on there?

DEFELICE: He told me. He said, "You got one on there."

LIPMAN: Now you claim only three hind quarters a month. That's pretty low, very low.

DEFELICE: I swear to you.

LIPMAN: I don't want you swearing to me. If it's three, I'll accept three. If it's three hundred, I want three hundred.

SCHROEDER: We want to know the figure.

DEFELICE: It's only three, boss.

(Editor's note: One after another the suspects entered the office and, under the pressure of Lipman's questioning, cracked.)

10:10 A.M.

DZEROVITCH: James Jackson was the big hitter.

11:09 A.M.

AL COVELLO: Somebody's fooling with the gas. They must weigh the truck empty instead of full, or with just enough fuel to get where they have to go, and the rest of the weight is extra meat. Or when they steam the trucks out each day they take all the hooks out—that can be a couple of hundred pounds of hooks—and they make up that weight with extra meat.

LIPMAN: Was Hubert Tinsley in on it?

COVELLO: Yes, he was.

VITALE: Did you ever steal meat?

COVELLO: Never. I knew it was going on, but I never stole nothing.

VITALE: Why didn't you come to Carl or to me?

COVELLO: You were a truck driver, Tony. Would you have gone to the boss?

VITALE: I am the boss.

SCHROEDER: Are you sure Hubert Tinsley was in on it?

COVELLO: Yes.

LIPMAN: Our man saw you stealing time, though. How many hours a week did you park your truck and go to a bar or a pool hall with other drivers?

COVELLO: I stole time, but I never stole no meat.

LIPMAN: About seven to ten hours a week, would you say?

COVELLO: Not that much.

LIPMAN: Let's say five then. Add that to his statement and have him sign it.

9:00 P.M.

We worked all day. We didn't even break for lunch. They have a stove in the corner of the office, and at lunch time Carl Schroeder went into the cooler, got some strip steaks, and had one of the secretaries cook them for us, so our lunch consisted of the steaks and some cokes. They were good steaks, but I told Carl that when he walks into the cooler and picks up a bunch of steaks without paying for them, he is in effect stealing those steaks. The men watch him do it and say to themselves, "If the boss can walk out of here with as many steaks as he wants, why can't I?"

I'll tell you how I broke Midnight Shadow. He wouldn't admit anything, so I cut my interrogation off fast, brought Johns from the other room, and said: "Here!"

At that point Shadow admitted to stealing a couple of hind quarters. He also told us that twenty or thirty men each night would steal whole knuckles of beef, roast them over the incinerator out back, and eat them before going home.

He said that that was all he knew and offered to be polygraphed. Now I knew the company had suspected him of stealing in the past and had sent him somewhere to be polygraphed. Before he took the test he had got drunk, and the results were inconclusive.

But today my own operator polygraphed him. Midnight Shadow went in there. He was awfully cocky. My man asked him only seven questions; most of which were control questions such as: "Do you live in Chicago, are you married, do you smoke?"

There were only two key questions; the first was, "Apart from what you've told us, do you know any others who are stealing?" The other key question was, "Have you stolen more meat than you've told us about?"

Well, on those two questions, the graph went right off the page. When I went back into the room, Midnight Shadow said: "I blew the machine right off that desk." He was proud of it. Then he began to talk, and he involved James Jackson for the first time. James Jackson, the ringleader.

I got Jackson to break in about four minutes. I saw that money ringing in the register—lots of chips there. I had that guy for three years of stealing. When Tony Vitale came in, he backed down to two years, and I finally increased it to two and a half years. Listen, it was safely a helluva lot more than that.

I tried to figure out how much the meat he had stolen would average per week; for the two-and-a-half year period, the total came to over $50,000. He signed a statement, and now the client will get at least that much money back from the bonding company, and there is a good chance of recovering twice as much. Today, we probably earned the client about $100,000.

By the middle of the day, everyone began naming our informant, Hubert Tinsley, so we polygraphed him. It showed that he had been stealing, but not too much, and that he had stopped quite a while ago. I saw that the client was so grateful to Hubert Tinsley for breaking open this case that he wanted to keep Hubert on, so I didn't proceed any further along that line. But my instincts had been right—I knew when I woke up this morning that he had to be involved in some way.

And then late in the afternoon, Agent Pete Peterson broke Shopovic. After I had broken Jackson, the client went over to where one of my agents was sitting with Shopovic and called out: "The game is over. You boys get your bonus. Your boss just struck paydirt, $50,000." My agent says Shopovic looked as if he had just been hit in the face with a wet pie. Pete then bore down on Shopovic, and after about two solid hours of interrogation, Shopovic signed a confession admitting the two transactions my agents had actually seen, no more.

How do I feel right this minute? I feel a helluva lot better than

I did last night or early this morning. Because I want to tell you right now, that when I got up this morning and reviewed the notes, I thought: Boy, if we make it, we're going to have a lot of prayer, because it looks sick.

We had nothing at all on James Jackson, for instance, and he was the ringleader. I was looking for straws. Jackson's facial expressions started to change when he realized the scope of the operation, the amount of money involved, and the fact that he hadn't really made that much money. Even though he admitted stealing close to $50,000 worth of meat, he probably didn't receive more than 10 percent of that amount himself.

In all, I interrogated thirteen people and got confessions from twelve.

Midnight Shadow admitted stealing about $10,000 worth of meat. That's thirteen weeks of stealing at so many hind quarters a week, a total of over $60,000 on those two guys. We got about $75,000 worth of confessions in all. The bonding company will have to pay up.

I'd say that we've accomplished a helluva lot here today. When the client takes you out to dinner after the deal, when he doesn't shove you off saying, well the job is done, forget it—that means he is happy. It is like you are taking out a woman, and you are through and you push her out of bed. That didn't happen today. We all went out to dinner and he paid. He was happy.

I'm happy too, but I'm also tired. I've been up since 5:30 A.M. and interrogating since before 8 A.M., but I feel revived right now. I won't replay all the arguments in my head in order to work out a way that I could have nailed Shopovic in one minute. As far as I'm concerned, it's history. I don't give a damn about it anymore, frankly. The hardest work for me was to fool around with those small-fry guys all afternoon, one after the other, when I had already nailed James Jackson and he was the guts of it.

I dictated the confessions that each of them was to sign, and then I walked out of the room before the guy signed it. The client was worried that if I left the room, the guy would think that he didn't have to sign. But I knew they would sign. They would sign because they knew I meant business. Two or three or four hours later they might not sign, but for the moment I had sold them on signing. They were still in a state of shock. They were guilty and I had caught them. Psychologically they were in my power. They would do whatever I told them to do.

What feeling do I have for these guys, especially somebody like James Jackson, a 51-year-old man with a family? He should have known better. They all should have known better. They didn't have to steal that money to live. Some of those men were earning a net of $280 to $290 a week.

James Jackson wasn't making that much, and looking at his face as he sat there in his bloody smock, I realized he was a broken man. It was sad. Why was he broken? Now you analyze this. He admitted more or less everything. Others who had admitted only a few dollars weren't broken at all. Take Shopovic, he wasn't broken because he admitted—finally—very little. A few hind quarters. Enough to fire him, and that's about all. He was proud of the fact that I didn't get him for all that he had taken. He felt he had put one over on me. He didn't indicate in any way that he was elated, but he was.

April 11

I interrogated a fellow named Hewitt this morning. He involved another truck driver. He revealed that he and this other driver would bring meat to James Jackson's house. Some of the extra meat Jackson was pushing onto the trucks would be brought to Jackson's garage and transferred to his car. They'd bring two or three rounds at a time, which represents 150-200 pounds at a crack. Yesterday Jackson told us nothing about this operation.

You should have seen James Jackson yesterday, this sad-eyed, 51-year-old family man. I almost felt sorry for him. Yesterday he was wearing a bloody white smock and a bloody apron, but today he came in dressed better than any of us. No bloody smock today. He was well dressed and composed, and later he went out to a bar with the informant, Hubert Tinsley, and asked, "Hubert, did you sign a statement?"

Hubert said, "No, I didn't." Hubert knew he was going to get reinstated, so he was smart enough to say he didn't sign a statement. So Jackson then mentioned somebody else who was in on the deal, a fellow who's related to Tony Vitale, the general manager. We polygraphed this guy, and he involved somebody else who was also stealing a little bit, not much. And this guy is the boss's relative!

Carl Schroeder, the vice-president, had a cousin working at Acme as a plant superintendent. I talked to this cousin about stealing, and we polygraphed him. He admitted that his father, who owns a little grocery store, comes in every other week and that he gives his father from ten to twenty pounds of extra meat. And this is Carl Schroeder's cousin! A lot of this is small time, but it adds up.

The clients felt pretty happy today. Carl said to me, "I'm going to find out where you get those cigars. I'm going to buy you a box of cigars."

Today a great many people—too many—seem to believe that in order to live well they have to steal, and that's part of the reason why thievery is rampant in our country. Today people have to have two automobiles. They used to be satisfied with one. They've got television. They see all the products they'd like to have but don't. Their children also learn about all these so-called essentials from watching TV. Their neighbors and classmates have these goods, so they bug their parents to death to buy them. So-and-so's got this, he's got that. The pressure gets to the father and to the mother too, if she's working. In today's factories, opportunity is all around them. Every bin and ware-house is like an open cash register. All they have to do is get in with somebody. Every day they're handling some kind of prod-uct that's salable. The companies are not putting in enough controls to stop the stealing. It's expensive to put in more guards and controls. And the minute you do put them in, your employees are going to figure out new ways of stealing because they have got used to living on higher incomes. The money they steal is used as extra salary. If the job pays $100 dollars a week and they steal $50 dollars a week, they're going to be living on $150 dollars. They're depending on it—they have to go on with it.

I nail about five hundred guys a year. Very little of this ever gets in the papers. Acme is not about to call up the Chicago *Tribune* and brag about how they were getting robbed, and I never tell the papers myself. When arrests are to be made, we let the police have the whole case. Once in a while the police will say that investigators were employed by the company, and in that way our names will be mentioned by the press.

In any case, thousands of people a year are caught by me and other agents like me, and those we catch are a drop in the bucket compared to what's going on in this country. The gen-eral public doesn't know about these thousands and thousands of people. They are very rarely prosecuted; they get fired, that's all, and then they go steal somewhere else. I think the Acme Packing Company will be safe for about six months. Then a new group will get in there and figure out a way to steal, and it will start all over again. Meanwhile, some of the people we didn't catch will quit that job and look for greener pastures where they can steal more easily, because they've got to have that extra money. They are living on it and they have to have it.

2.   Bayview, Arkansas:
A Pants Factory Case

•

Try walking out unnoticed with 180 pairs of pants on your person

April 12

I'm driving out to the Meyer Clothing Factory in Bayview, Arkansas. Yesterday in Chicago it was 39 degrees, but here spring is well along. The fields are green, the leaves are almost out, and in the towns the azaleas are blooming.

The case is as follows. About five weeks ago we put an agent into this factory. There has been a lot of stealing going on, and our agent found out that a 50-year-old black janitor named Howie McNeil was doing a lot of it. We investigated Howie McNeil and found that he had just bought a new house, a new car, and a new pickup truck.

Our agent, whose car we had provided with Louisiana license plates, asked Howie to get him some merchandise. Howie promptly sold him two cartons of stolen pants. I have those cartons in this car right now. One of the cartons is so big it fills up the trunk. The other is a little smaller, but we could barely get it into the back seat.

Now Howie McNeil is no angel. We know that he was involved with bootleggers for years. At some point he got wind of our agent and went to his boss, a man named Winstead Snopes, and said: "That man from Louisiana, he is a thief. He try to get Howie to steal." Very alarmed, Snopes called up the home office. Were we sure of our agent and so forth? Of course we were sure of him.

Anyway, to soothe Snopes, we asked him to mark some bills and give them to our agent, which he did. Our agent then made another buy from McNeil, paying him with the marked bills. A few minutes later Snopes came by and the agent said: "I just gave McNeil the marked bills."

So Snopes went running over to where McNeil was working and said: "Say, Howie, I have an important buyer coming in today, I want you to work extra hard and get these aisles cleaned up. By the way, McNeil, can you change a $10 bill for me?"

Howie said he didn't have change.

Snopes said, "Can you change $5, then?"

So Howie hauls out seven dollar bills, all marked, and hands them to Snopes in exchange for the five. I don't know whether this encounter with Snopes scared him, or what. Snopes went back into his office, checked that they were all marked bills, and locked them in his drawer. He later went out and said: "You gave me two dollars too much, Howie." And gave him back two other bills.

So we have a beautiful case against Howie McNeil—two big buys of over a hundred pairs of pants, plus the marked bills. A cinch deal. I'll interrogate McNeil and probably break him within two minutes. Two minutes after that I'll have his signed confession.

Now I'm in the car driving away.

I met with Mr. Snopes in his office. He's a man about 45, very nervous, his eyes blinking all the time. First thing, he gets out the marked bills and shows them to me. He can't believe it. Howie McNeil is one of his oldest and most trusted employees.

Honest Howie. In fact, he doesn't want to believe it. Am I sure our agent is okay? Maybe our agent was the thief. Howie wouldn't steal; Snopes is sure of that.

While he went to get Howie, I looked into the factory. It's an enormous low-ceilinged place with 450 employees. Most of them are women at sewing machines. The place hums with the sewing machines. Each woman does one little task over and over again. I stood watching a woman who sews only the inside seam of the left pants leg. There's a rig on either side of her machine, so she grasps two pieces of material, runs them through the machine, and then grasps two more.

I couldn't do a job like that.

It took Snopes a long time to find Howie McNeil, and when he did find him, Howie was in an area where he wasn't supposed to be. It's possible that he almost caught Howie in the act of stealing.

When he got into the office with me, Howie was ready for anything. The marked money was a cold deal, and I didn't see how he could escape. Actually, Snopes could have had him arrested, and I think he could have made it stick.

However, when I told Howie who I was and informed him that we had him cold for stealing, he denied it. He just stood there and lied, declaring that it was the man from Louisiana, meaning our agent, who was the thief. According to Howie, this man had tried to get him to steal, but Howie never wanted any of that.

He went on lying. I called Mr. Snopes in, and we talked about the marked bills. According to Howie, the agent planted those bills on him. I could see that Snopes wanted to believe him. In fact, he did believe him. Howie sat there chewing on a toothpick. He chewed that toothpick to bits, sweating and lying. He said he would take a lie detector test and that it would show he was telling the truth.

After about twenty minutes I saw there was no point going

on. I had them take Howie to another room and asked to see one of the shipping clerks, Billy Joe Morrow, whom we had nothing on. Nothing at all. Our agent had heard his name mentioned once as a guy who was stealing pants.

Now there is no question about the fact that stolen pants are leaving that factory. Snopes could go bankrupt any minute. Actually, the whole town could go bankrupt. Bayview isn't very large, and this one factory practically supports the entire economy of the town.

Billy Joe Morrow sat down across the desk; he was a nice-looking, fair-haired young fellow. I thought it would take only a few minutes to move him, and that's exactly what it took. He told me he lived with his mother. His father had died recently, and Mr. Snopes had gone to bat for him and got him released from the army after only seven months' service. Snopes put him back in the factory so he could support his mother. But did this boy show any gratitude? None at all.

I told Billy that I knew he was getting pants and that I knew he had been getting them for about four months. His face turned red, then white. He admitted he had taken a few pairs here and there. I told him I might make a further investigation and find out that he hadn't told the whole truth. Then his opportunity to work this out would be gone. So he admitted that he had started stealing six months after he came to work in the shipping department, and he had been working there three years. Then we determined how many pairs he had taken.

I went through the names of everybody in the shipping department, asking Billy Joe for yes or no answers, and he named eleven of twenty-three people. About 50 percent of the employees of that area were stealing, according to Billy. I asked him to tell me how they were getting the pants out of the factory. Instead of telling me, he stood up, took a pair of pants out of a box beside Snopes' desk, and showed me. It was impressive. He then signed the following statement: "I, Billy Joe Mor-

row, having been informed that I do not have to make a statement, nonetheless make the following statement: I am 20 years
of age, single, live with my mother, Sarah Morrow, Route 1,
Bayview, Arkansas. I have a high school education. I started to
work for Meyer Clothing Factory about three years ago but was
in service between June and December 1970. About six months
after I came to work here I started taking pants for my own
personal use and benefit. I have taken as many as two pairs a
day and as many as four to five pairs in a week. Some weeks I
didn't take anything. If I happened to get pants that were not
my size, I sold them to relatives at $2.50 a pair. I did not keep
a record of the pants I took, but I would estimate that I got
about 180 pairs. The following people who worked in the area
where I do have taken out pants—Toby Tobias, Neil Morgan,
Woodrow Wilkins, John Gittens, Clyde Smith, Adam Powers,
Neville Newton, Joseph Grant, Homer Short, Roswell Roy.
These people, including myself, take the pants out at lunch time
or about 4 P.M. by folding them to the size of a thick magazine
and tucking them into our pants behind the fly. That is one way.
Another is to put them into the seat of the pants. It makes a very
slight bulge that can barely be seen. You then pass the guard on
the outside of the crowd so that there are people between him
and you and he does not get a good look at you. Sometimes men
wear them out under their own pants, but very few, because
putting them on takes too long. You can fold the pants against
the abdomen very much more quickly, in less than five seconds.

"I have not been promised anything.

"This statement is true and correct to the best of my knowledge and belief and made in the presence of Mark Lipman,
private investigator, and Winstead Snopes."

Five seconds is about what it took him to make that pair of
pants disappear. He was wearing tight Levi's, and he had his fly
unzipped and the stolen pants against his abdomen and his fly

zipped up again faster than you would believe. And even though his Levi's were tight, you couldn't really tell there was a second pair of pants hidden under them.

Snopes had come back into the office by this time, and it made him sick to watch this. Morrow claimed everybody was stealing. Basically, the reason he informed on most of the men working with him was that he did not want us to think he was the only crook in the place. His eyes blinking, Snopes listened to him. It was painful to watch. Morrow said that men come to work in old pants, strip them off, and put a new pair on. Snopes said he knew about that. On his filing cabinet he had a pair of dungarees with the seat torn, which he had found that morning under some boxes. Obviously somebody had hidden them and gone out with new pants on. Worn-out pants are found hidden in the factory all the time. Many of the women take out pants or parts of pants—whatever parts they happen to be working on—in their handbags. They all have sewing machines at home. They meet outside, exchange pieces, and go home to sew up a new pair of pants. They call it a buddy system.

So we had Morrow there, looking scared, and Snopes with his eyes blinking, and then Snopes began to make this passionate speech to Morrow about how tight the competition is, how little money the factory is making. He said the factory could go broke at any time. He told Morrow that he had gone to a thread manufacturer and offered him the entire business from his factory, amounting to about $5 million worth of thread, if he could have a rebate of only 5 percent. The thread manufacturer refused him.

These workers all think the owners are making a fortune; instead, the owners are being squeezed out, just like everybody else. If the thread manufacturer can throw away $5 million worth of business over a 5 percent rebate, then you know he doesn't have any profit margin to speak of either.

Manufacturers are being squeezed by prices, by competition,

and by theft. Theft is a tremendous factor. This boy Morrow admitted to stealing pants worth over $1,500 wholesale, and he's one of eleven in his department who we know are stealing. Morrow has probably stolen more than he admitted to, and some of the others have probably stolen more than Morrow. If you apply the percentage of thieves in Morrow's department to the entire staff, then you have two hundred employees robbing the owner.

What Snopes did, after this speech, was to send Morrow back to work. The speech might have some effect on Morrow. If Snopes made the same speech to the entire factory, it might have some effect on the others, but not much. Those people are out there working machines, sewing the left pants leg or whatever, one tiny little job, and they have no contact with Snopes' problems. That's part of the reason people are stealing from factories. Snopes pays Morrow $2.30 an hour, which is a lot of money in rural Arkansas. It's about 75 cents more than the other local garment factories are paying, so paying better wages certainly doesn't stop the stealing. Money is not the answer. The people don't feel they're stealing from Snopes; they feel as if they're stealing from a row of machines.

So Snopes let Morrow go. Morrow didn't tell us half the truth. He probably picked up 500 pairs, not 180, and he didn't sell 180 pairs to his relatives. How many relatives can he have? He was selling them somewhere, but I didn't go after him on that point. I saw that Snopes wanted to keep him, to send him back to the shipping department as a stool pigeon. But Snopes will not go after the other boys. He has to get the work out, and putting pressure on the other boys would stir up the organization. He'd have to fire them all.

But Billy Joe is scared now. He knows that the next time he's caught today's confession will be on file. He might go to jail. It's like a suspended sentence—we have put him on probation. He's lucky to get off this easily.

So now I'm driving away and I'm aggravated that I didn't break Howie McNeil. The way I see it, the client ruined this case. Howie suspected our agent was fishy and denounced him to Snopes as a thief. Snopes then built him up to Howie as a probable thief whom they were watching, and this ruined the element of surprise and gave Howie a perfect out. He could blame everything on our agent. Snopes is going to bring Howie to our Memphis office to be polygraphed. We'll see what that shows. We are also going to polygraph our own agent.

A 50-year-old uneducated man like Howie McNeil, who's been lying all his life, is always a tough subject. A boy like Billy Joe Morrow, properly raised with some moral principles, is a pushover. Because he's guilty, and he knows that I know he's guilty, he admits it. His conscience forces him to confess. However, moral principles don't prevent the stealing in the first place.

Twenty years ago I figured that three out of every ten employees were stealing from the company. Today I figure it's seven out of ten. Some steal occasionally and the rest steal regularly. I get this impression from the tremendous expansion in our business—we don't do any advertising; we get all our clients through referrals—and from the fact that we now catch so many more people in each place.

There is no morality in this country today. Everyone can see that no one is obeying the law. People feel: "So what if I get caught, the case won't come up for three years, and even then I have a fifty-fifty chance of beating it." People know what's going on. They read the papers. They read about the war and the riots.

All an owner can do is to put more controls in his plant to cut down on the opportunity to steal. But controls only slow down thefts—anyone who really wants to steal is very inventive. In one case I investigated, I found out that guys were entering a liquor store wearing cowboy boots—guys with thin calves and wide boots. They would shove half-pint bottles into the top of the boots, two to each leg, walk out, put the liquor in their car, and walk back in again. Also, I once caught a woman who would walk into a typewriter place, make a sort of half squat over a typewriter, pick it up with her knees or thighs, and walk out with it under her skirt. With a typewriter between her legs, she could walk perfectly. Unbelievable. I also caught a woman who could walk out with six or eight cartons of cigarettes clutched between her legs—she actually had callouses on her thighs. Another woman used to shoplift frozen meat that way. One day a frozen chicken got too cold for her, and just as she was walking past the cashier, she had to let go of it. It hit the floor with a thud, rolling, and she just kept walking. There was also the automotive plant where I broke a case; guys were stealing spark plugs and other small parts by taping them around their legs with masking tape and then just walking out with them at night.

Sometimes when I break a case, I give advice to the owner. One thing I always tell him is that he has got to start screening his employees, get their backgrounds, check up on them. Employers think that because the job is menial they don't have to screen the man they offer it to.

I suggested to Snopes that he try closed-circuit TV. He could install a lot of extra cameras that are dummies. It's all psychology anyway. You've got to let the employees know they're being watched.

Of course, they have closed-circuit TV all over the Acme meat-packing plant in Chicago, and you know how much good that did. They had eight TV monitors in the office, with no one watching any of them. The salesmen in there were all too busy selling. Some of those cameras fanned around, and Midnight Shadow said that as soon as the camera swung off you, you could do anything you wanted. It's stupid to have moving cameras.

Before leaving the Meyer Clothing Factory, I shook hands

with Morrow. Some of the people who work for me react adversely to these people, but I never do. Usually I look at one of these subjects and think, "He's just a fool."

When I get a young person between 18 and 25, I feel sorry for him. I always use the expression "Every dog's entitled to one bite." After I get a confession, I like to give a lecture. "You've done this thing and been caught, but you've opened up your heart and told us everything. I want you now to go out and get a job and forget about this thing. Don't keep your head down. You should keep your head high and do a good job. Let today be a lesson to you. The next time you have an opportunity to steal, think about today. Remember that next time you may not run into a guy like me, who is giving you a break. I'm putting you on probation, just like the courts. But the next time you get caught, they're going to check your record with your former employer. They'll find out about today. So think about it, think about your family, your children, not only about yourself. The people in your family are going to be the ones who suffer."

I usually do that with young kids. But after someone is 25 or 30 years old, I have no regard for him at all. None. He should know better, but he gets involved and steals. I don't have any respect for people like that.

I once investigated a case in Lebanon, Pennsylvania. It was one of the oldest shirt companies in the country. They had information that a 50-year-old man was stealing. He had worked for them for thirty-five years. We sent an agent there who found that this man was taking mail orders for his own profit but that he had made the mistake of tearing up the correspondence and throwing it in his wastebasket. We knew exactly where he was selling, how much he was selling.

When I questioned him, he admitted to about $11,000 in thefts. He had $9,000 in the bank. We went to the bank and got the money right there and then. He said that his wife was going through menopause and that he was having problems with her. Every time he got home at night, they argued. He was so disgusted that he started playing poker two or three nights a week just to get away from the house. He had never before played in his life, and he lost heavily.

This was a situation in which you could have some feeling for the guy. So I telephoned the client in New York. I told him that this man was a member of the city council and had been a member of the volunteer fire department. Because he had had a lot of problems in the last three or four years, he had started to steal. I said, "I would like to have him finish out the week so that no one in the community will know he was fired." It's a town of only 2,500 people. I pointed out that the man had paid back nearly all the money that he'd taken.

The New York attorney and the president of the company agreed to let the man finish out the week. I said, "He's not going to take anything in the next two or three days. Let him leave for some invented reason so he won't be hurt in the community. He's suffering enough now."

That night at my hotel I received a telephone call from one of their supervisors. He said, "They tell me that you're letting this guy work the rest of the week?"

I answered, *"I'm* not letting him work the rest of the week. I got permission from the company."

He said, "The guy's a thief. And he's fired as of right now, and I'm not going to let him in the building tomorrow."

I said, "Well, you ought to clear it with New York."

He said, "I have the authority to do it."

I said, "Now, I'm Jewish, and you're Christian. Did you ever hear of Jesus Christ?"

"Yes."

I said, "Do you know what the word compassion means?" And I hung up.

He did fire the man. But he made me so mad, he got me so angry, I just couldn't stand it. There are times when you must have compassion.

April 28

We called in James Knotts, our agent from the Meyer Clothing Factory case, the so-called thief from Louisiana, to polygraph him. I told him what had happened, that I had been unable to break Howie McNeil and that McNeil had accused him of being a thief and a liar.

"I assume that everything you told us, everything you wrote in your reports, was true," I said.

He said: "Yes, it was."

"You did buy that stolen merchandise from Howie McNeil?"

"Yes I did."

"I am going to ask you to be polygraphed. Not because I suspect you, but because we need to reassure the client."

He was cool as could be. He said: "Go ahead and polygraph me."

We did. He was clean as a whistle. Every word he said was true. Arrangements are now being made to bring McNeil here to be polygraphed. I hope to clean this case up in the next day or two.

May 25

Howie McNeil has never come in to be polygraphed.

If they had polygraphed him, they would have been obliged to fire him. The owner, Winstead Snopes, has a paternalistic attitude toward Howie, his employee for over twenty years. He figures he isn't guilty, couldn't possibly be guilty; and even if he is guilty, Snopes feels he won't steal anymore. I am deducing all of this. Snopes never actually stated his position—he just made one excuse after another as to why he couldn't bring McNeil in to be polygraphed.

I don't think this man, this 50-year-old Howie McNeil will ever stop stealing.

3. The Man from Mark Lipman

•

A modern private investigator works coast to coast

I was the tenth of ten children. Three older brothers were in the finance business in Philadelphia when I joined them after completing a degree in accounting at Temple University. I started by making investigations of credit and some searches for people who had skipped town. That was my background in investigation when in 1933 I applied for and was granted a detective's license in Philadelphia.

In 1934 a lawyer sent me to Houston, Texas, to complete an investigation of an estate. I was impressed with the Southwest. I had a friend who wanted to obtain a divorce from his wife and finally decided to go to Little Rock, Arkansas. In 1935 you could get a ninety-day divorce there. My friend gave up his job, hoping to get started in a new area of the country. I began to consider this, too. I could get away from family and a business which, while it was profitable, was not progressive. No one was particularly interested in developing it. And being the youngest, not being able to do too much with three older brothers, I decided to go to Little Rock—not even knowing where it was, not even bothering to look it up on the map.

As we drove down, I was wondering if a living could be made

there. We began passing all those broken-down homes that black people were living in, little shanties sitting on stilts. I looked out the window and thought: "Can I make a living here?" I didn't have any money. I had $100, and I had left my wife $100. We had placed our things in storage, and she had gone to New York City to live with her folks temporarily. It was a gamble; I had been making about $75 a week, which was very good money in 1935.

The day of my arrival in Little Rock was March 14, 1935. I rented P.O. Box No. 82. I still have the same box. I don't get much mail there, but I still keep it. After a short time, I left Little Rock to go to Texas to see if I could line up some work in the finance business. Nothing was available there either, so I returned to Little Rock. There was a letter waiting—my father had passed away suddenly. I called my folks. I knew that if I returned to Philadelphia—the funeral was already over—I would stay there.

And so, being further depressed at the loss of my father, I started going around to corporation lawyers in an attempt to get some investigative work. My investigative skills were very limited. One of the men I went to see was an insurance adjuster named Earl Snapp. He said he was getting $15 a day from an insurance company to make a certain investigation in a case they were going to lose anyway. "I will give you $7.50 a day to make this investigation for me, and I'll pay your expenses as well. If you work ten days on this, you'll make $75. I don't know a thing about you—you might be a crook. You look honest. What can I lose? We're going to lose the case anyway."

I took the job sometime in April. I went to Hot Springs to meet a group of attorneys who represented the Hardware Mutual Casualty Co., who had the coverage of a department store. A woman claimed that she had been in a department store elevator and had fallen, hurting her back. It developed that she was close to the mayor of Hot Springs, Leo McLaughlin.

He was a boss mayor; he ran the complete operation. At that time Hot Springs was wide open. There was gambling in the streets, and all the cigar stores on Central Avenue had punch boards. You could make bets on horses. Racketeers, gunmen, and bookies would all go down and hide out there.

These attorneys wanted me to investigate this woman who alleged a back injury and who said she could not do anything because of her injury. After contacting the neighbors, finding out about her church affiliation, and talking to a lot of people, many of whom had city jobs and were afraid to say anything, I developed proof that the woman had no back injury at all. I even got signed statements to that effect. I then reported back to the attorneys, who were very pleased. Mr. Snapp was pleased, too, but thought it was a wasted effort. My witnesses would never show up for trial, he said.

At the attorneys' office the questions about the investigation were directed to me, and I finally made a suggestion. I said, "If you think this political situation in Hot Springs is so bad that they will scare or fix any witnesses we subpoena, then why don't you let me bring all of my people in as surprise witnesses? I think I have them sold on the idea of telling the truth. Let me be responsible for bringing them in. You don't have anything to lose. You might as well try it."

They agreed to do it. So I went back to my witnesses. They were all people who lived near the woman and knew her, and I had picked the most moral people I could find, ministers and so forth. I convinced them that if ten people all testified that they had seen the woman sweeping her stoop, carrying bags of groceries, and so on, then no one would be made a scapegoat. There was no reason to be scared if all of them stuck together and told the truth.

Every witness that I had lined up, from the Episcopal minister to neighbors, was brought into court. They all testified truthfully. There were supposed to be certain fixed people on the jury. The trial resulted in a hung jury. No one could agree. It was a moral victory, that's all. But the word went out about me, and I started to get some business. It was rough. From April to September I averaged about $50 a month, but every case I worked on resulted in either a hung jury or a guilty verdict.

I became acquainted with a very dynamic person, Grover T. Owens, who headed a large law firm. He had good men in the firm. He raised a lot of hell, demanded a lot, but he was a good man. It took me two months to get business from him. He finally gave me one job, I think because he felt sorry for me, a guy coming down from Philadelphia, still wearing a winter suit. It was unbelievably hot, over 100 degrees every day in May, and there was no air-conditioning at that time. I had no automobile either. I would hitchhike, take buses, and take trains. Many of the people I had to investigate lived in the country. I would walk over gravel roads for miles at a time. I wasn't used to that kind of stuff.

I will tell you one thing. When you come down South and you are from the North, southerners think you are a wise guy just because you speak differently. The fact that I was broke and hungry was my greatest asset. And that is what I have been teaching my agents ever since that time. Be humble. Act dumb. Don't be a wise guy. If people feel sorry for you, you will get a lot of information. But if you're going to act like a big shot, forget it. These southerners could look at me and know that I was fighting, and that is why I was successful from the start at getting information from them. I could get information from anyone.

Getting back to Grover T. Owens, he gave me a case to investigate in Texarkana, about 125 miles from Little Rock. He gave me a $25 expense check and took $25 cash out of his pocket and said, "Here, give this to your wife. If you turn out to be a sour ball, that's all right, I've lost it. Leave that money with your wife so that she can buy groceries and you won't have to worry about anything." This was after my wife had arrived from New York on May 6. The bus fare was $25 from New York, and the ride took over forty hours.

I went to Texarkana to make the investigation. Really, no investigation was needed. I read briefs of state supreme court appeals and federal court appeals. I really felt that Mr. Owens was trying to do me a favor. I didn't think an investigation was needed, but I did a creditable job of reading supreme court and federal court appeals. I did more and more work for him, and he was so impressed with my work that today I still represent many clients to whom I was introduced by Mr. Owens. Everyone in this world, I don't care who he is, needs a push sometime in his life. Grover Owens was the man who gave me that push. But making a living, month after month, was tough. Then came a strange shoplifting case. This was my first big success.

A woman came into a supermarket on a Monday morning. There was another woman with her, and they had parked their car across the street. There were no other customers in the store. One of the women picked up a bottle of Welch's grape juice worth about 49 cents and walked right out past the cashier with it. She held it up right in front of him as she walked out.

He was so provoked that he went out into the street after her. She was just getting into her car. He said, "You didn't pay for that grape juice."

The second women had gotten into the car too. There was a bag of groceries sitting on the floor between them. The cashier watched her put the grape juice into that bag. He said, "You need to pay me."

She said, "I didn't get any grape juice from you. I've had those groceries since last Saturday."

He said, "I'm calling the cops."

She said, "Go ahead."

The man should have had sense enough to know it was a setup. But he didn't, and when the police came he had that woman arrested. The case came up in the city court a few days later. The first woman testified she had bought that grape juice the previous Saturday. The second woman verified this. The first woman's husband, who was in the naval reserve, testified that he and his wife had bought those groceries the previous Saturday—not at this store but at some other store—and then had gone to a party and left them in the car.

The judge had no choice but to throw the case out, and the woman and her husband sued the grocery chain for $50,000.

Mr. Owens assigned me to that case, saying: "Find out everything you can about these two women. Don't stop at anything. This is a frame, we know it's a frame. Get everything there is."

I started investigating. I found out that both women had collected money from Sears, Montgomery Ward, and many other local department stores. They had alleged falls on escalators or stairs. They had made every phony claim you can imagine, and rather than start a lawsuit the stores had paid them off.

I dug into this case so deeply that I located a Mrs. Winston, who formerly lived with the woman who had stolen the grape juice. They were now on the outs with each other. Mrs. Winston told me: "If you look up her record about eight or nine years ago, you'll find that an insurance company paid a fire loss. She set the fire herself after first removing all the good stuff that was inside. I was in the room when she did it. The house and contents were a total loss, and the insurance company paid off."

I found out that this woman, even though married, was a prostitute in a town twenty-four miles from Little Rock. The woman who had been in the car with her was also married and was also a prostitute.

We went to trial, and we won that case. The foreman of the jury, after announcing the verdict, said: "This is the filthiest thing I've ever heard. I'm going home to take a bath."

A copy of my report was later sent to every insurance company in the United States by their casualty claim association.

The names of those women went into their central phony claims index.

After that case I never had to worry about business. Within a year after my arrival in Little Rock, I had to hire a young lawyer to help me handle the business.

My son Ira was born, and he entered the business at an early age. By the time he was 13, I had a number of contracts with stores—both department stores and small shops—who were complaining about dishonest salesclerks and cashiers. Sometimes I sent Ira into places to make small purchases so that we could verify that these sales were being rung up. Who would ever suspect that such a child was, in effect, an undercover agent? We caught a lot of dishonest clerks that way.

Ira grew into a great salesman. He could sell Mark Lipman Service to almost anybody. He was so successful that he realized before I did that there was an explosion of stealing going on in the country. He said we should start a security-guard service. Reluctantly I agreed, and we called the new firm Guardsmark. But I didn't have time to worry about it, and Ira was only in his early 20's.

But that was less than ten years ago. By the time he was 30, Guardsmark was the sixth biggest guard service in the country, Ira was a millionaire, and he had bought me out. Mark Lipman Service is now a division of Guardsmark, and I work, in effect, for my own son. He sends me business, and I send him business, which I mention only to indicate how much business there is around. Ira says in his magazine ads for Guardsmark that the biggest business in the country today by far is employee stealing, and I agree with him.

At this time I have about eighty agents working for Mark Lipman Service. We have moved our main office to Memphis, and we have branch offices in New York, Los Angeles, and various other cities. Altogether we handle between sixty and eighty cases at once. But I still do almost all the interrogations myself.

This is possible because I have an exceptionally good man running this office for me, W. R. McGraw.

McGraw started with us in 1955 as an undercover agent in Little Rock. Then I developed him into the shopping crew, and from there to a supervisor of a shopping crew. Then he developed into a supervising agent, then a hiring agent. In 1963 we gave him 8% interest in the business. We just gave it to him, he never asked for it. He's loyal, dependable. I used to raise plenty of hell with him, bawl him out unmercifully. But he took it.

He's married, has three children. No problems, no divorce, no nothing, clean as a hound's tooth. Never asked for a raise in his life. Never asked for anything. He never complained, and that's very unusual. He went to Little Rock University, and he's a classical pianist too. Recently a friend said to me, "I saw your man McGraw sit down at the piano in the mezzanine of the Lafayette Hotel and he had an audience, he was that good." Mac even has a stereo in his office, and in the evening, when everybody's gone, he may listen to some of his symphony records.

We have to screen and check thirty applicants before we hire a single agent. Sometimes we must make a client wait two to three weeks before we can find the proper person to send him. The man from Mark Lipman is the type of man who can blend into an operation. He can do the job he is asked to do and will work harder than anybody else. He will gain the confidence of the other employees. He will work two or three weeks before he even asks anybody any questions. He is not a smart guy, he's a dummy as far as they're concerned, and he gains their confidence and goodwill and finds out what's going on in a plant. He may even be observing irregularities, but he's not going to do anything about them at first. We don't believe in jumping the gun. We don't show our hand the minute we see a guy stealing one pencil or one tie or one shirt.

We have to hire agents with specific skills. A couple of days ago a client asked us to send him a middle-aged white tailor. Impossible. What we did find, after about a hundred phone calls, was a 27-year-old black tailor who was willing to work for us in New York. When he came in yesterday, he was wearing a suit that he had cut from a bolt, laid out, and made himself. He and his brother are partners and since business is slow, he is able to leave. We have this job for him in an exclusive men's store on Madison Avenue where someone is stealing.

Once we hire this man as a tailor, we keep him. His next job may be something else entirely. We don't hire part-time employees. If he wants to go back to being a tailor later, that's fine, but we hire him with the idea of keeping him even though he may not get another tailoring assignment from us for the next twenty years.

His training will begin with studying actual cases, old cases, which will show him how to prepare a report, what the contents of the report are, and how agents handle themselves under certain situations. Then we'll give him a question-and-answer session. We won't let him out until he answers every question perfectly. This particular tailor will be trained for three days. Training usually takes from a week to ten days. On his arrival in New York he will have to use his own initiative in finding a place to live.

Our tailor can't let the men he will be working with know that he is a very good tailor, because then he will not get any information from them. If they think he is good, they are liable to be jealous. He has to be low man on the totem pole. He has to ask them questions. How have they been sewing these cuffs, or whatever it is? In this way, he will be able to cultivate a friendship with these people and blend in with them. They will start feeling sorry for him and give him further information. But if they think he knows more than they do, he won't get a damn thing. He has to be a smart guy but act like a dummy. All our assignments work this way.

The tailor is aware that he is to be both a tailor and an investigator. He will be paid $200 a week in New York, which is actually a raise for him. As an agent he will have a basic salary of about $130 a week. If he makes less than this on some job, we make up the difference. And we pay his subsistence. If we put him in a job at about $200 a week, which is more than his guarantee, he keeps that amount and we give him between $25 and $50 a week extra for his reports. His subsistence, if he is away from home, remains the same. Sometimes, if an agent breaks a big case, he gets a bonus. If he works overtime, he gets paid at overtime rates.

I don't know how other agencies work. Perhaps some of them work as we do, perhaps none of them do. But with us everything is geared toward interrogation—if we catch a single guy, we may come out with six or seven accomplices.

We check out each new agent. We check their backgrounds and their former employers, and before we hire them we polygraph them. Even if the whole investigation is excellent and the guy looks great, we still must polygraph him before he goes out. The polygraph examiner will ask whether he has held back any information on his background, whether he has ever been arrested; we also ask whether he intends to work here permanently. In addition, we send everybody through the police department to be fingerprinted, and these prints are checked out by the FBI. This is done to make certain that no agent has a criminal background. I do not believe that it takes a thief to catch a thief. I will not hire a man who has a record. It's not that I don't believe he doesn't deserve another chance. That might be all right if he's selling buttons. But when we're dealing with people who have to report on other people, we must be sure of our men.

Our agents work under a false identity, which is very difficult to do. The agent uses his own name, but one day he may work in a furniture factory, the next day as an auditor, and the next day as something else. He may go from Chicago to New York to Montana to New Orleans. He sometimes gets tired of that; he never builds any roots.

Many times the client will want to keep our agent because he's such a good worker. After Agent Coleman broke a frozen food case, the client wanted to keep him permanently. Well, that's strictly up to our agent, and Coleman decided he would stay with us. The client gave him a $100 tip because he was so appreciative. That's a rarity, but it does happen from time to time.

The majority of our agents work as truck drivers, stock sorters, truck loaders, or helpers on trucks.

We also have about five female agents. Very difficult to handle. Very difficult. But some jobs call for a female. If you've got a garment plant where the seamstresses are stealing, you're probably better off putting a female agent in there. Or you might have to put in a female because there is no turnover among the male employees. You would have to create a position for a male agent, and that in itself would label him. The trouble with female agents is that they may fall in love with the male employee who is their subject. If a female agent falls in love with a male subject, then we're through, because she's going to tell him what she's doing. A male agent doesn't generally do that. For example, I can tell you about a case where I got a complete double cross.

This case had to do with a furniture warehouse in Baton Rouge, Louisiana, which had a $19,000 shortage. It was a certified inventory shortage. We tried many ways to catch the warehouse superintendent, whom we were really suspicious of. We tried to make purchases from him; we put an agent to work there. But we never could get anything on him. They told me that he was a man about 50 years old. He was always running around with young girls, although he was married, so I figured that he could be had.

We had a really beautiful girl working for us. All I wanted her to do was get an apartment and have him fill that apartment with stolen furniture. I said, "I do not want you to go to bed with this guy. Under no circumstances." I meant this. Not so much for reasons of morality as to protect the case. I knew the danger involved.

She said, "I wouldn't fool around with a 50-year-old man anyway."

I said: "All right, I'll tell you what to do. This superintendent has a habit of stepping outside during the day. About three blocks from the warehouse there's a garment factory. About two o'clock in the afternoon I want you to walk by the warehouse as if you're looking for this garment plant. He'll come out. If he doesn't, try the same thing thirty minutes later. When he does come out, say to him, 'Am I on the right street? I'm looking for this garment company that's located around here, I don't know where.' "

So she did that. Sure enough the superintendent came out, and she talked to him. He told her where the garment plant was, Then he said: "Now honey, if you don't get that job, come right back here and I'll take care of you."

Well she went up there, was gone for about an hour, then came back. He saw her and came running out. He said, "How'd you do?"

She said, "They weren't hiring anybody right now."

He asked her how her finances were, and she told him she was running low on money. So he said, "You go over to this hotel (he told her where it was) and wait there in the lobby. About

4:30 I'll come over there, and I'll get you an apartment and get you fixed up."

He did get her an apartment and she got friendly with him. There's always the danger of the female agent going to bed with her subject. It's all chemistry, and she only has to fall in love with him for one night. So I give all my female agents the same lecture. This girl got nothing extra in the way of lectures from me, and I really figured she was safe. She was from a good family, only 23 years old, and a really beautiful girl; and this superintendent was over 50 and a warehouseman. He didn't even dress well. I figured she could flirt with him and con him, and because of his age he'd fall for her and begin to give her furniture. She wouldn't have to do anything in return but blink her eyes at him. She could play the coy virgin and hold him off until I was ready to make my interrogation. And if this doesn't seem ethical, my answer is that this guy was a thief. He'd been stealing furniture for years, and I was out to nail him any way I could. Would it have been more ethical to draw the line and leave him there?

He visited her every day. I don't know what they did there, but anyway he visited her, and he brought furniture, furniture, furniture. We checked all the tickets, and we didn't find any sales recorded for this furniture. We thought we had a good case. One of the controllers and I flew to Baton Rouge to question the guy. Before we questioned him, we checked the tickets again. This time there were receipts for all the furniture, every piece. They had been put there the day before.

I had made the mistake of telling my female agent that I was coming down the next day to interrogate the superintendent. A week had already elapsed and no receipts for that furniture had come in, so I thought she was all right, that everything was fine.

The superintendent was looking down my throat when I questioned him. I knew we shouldn't question him, but we were there. I asked why these tickets hadn't been recorded until a week later. We knew we were double-crossed. He simply denied any wrongdoing.

So that case was a bust. The client was disturbed. I was disturbed. About six months later, I got a phone call from the client. "I want to tell you the truth, Mark. Another company came in here after you and told us they had a good man, familiar with furniture, and that we ought to put this man to work. So we did. He hasn't gotten anything. Now we have a telephone call telling us that some of our furniture is in an employment agency downtown, and we checked and found that we haven't sold this employment agency anything. It is supposed to have been put in there by our warehouse superintendent."

Since the client had another company working for him, I suggested he ask them to make the interrogation. They flew a man in from Dallas, and he got a confession which was taken on a very rough piece of paper, in pencil, in which the superintendent admitted having sold one chair. He didn't admit anything else. That's all they had, and it wasn't good enough.

The client then asked me, "What do you think we ought to do?"

We dispatched a couple of men. We followed the employment agency lead and other leads, and we came up with quite a bit of merchandise that the superintendent had stolen and sold.

Then I went in and questioned him. The first thing I said was, "I was double-crossed on that last deal. You knew that girl was my agent, but it's a different ball game right now. Now we've got you cold. Not only that, we know exactly how long you're stealing and how much is involved. I can't prove $19,000, which is what you actually took, but we've got you for $12,000."

I started mentioning a couple of his deals, then said: "If I have to go any further you're not going to get a break." The net result was that I obtained a long-winded statement for $12,000. The bonding company paid off the $19,000.

As for the girl, he admitted that they had had intimate relations and that she had told him I was coming to interrogate him. I fired the girl. I told her what had happened there. What she had sold me out for was the furniture that he had stolen for her. She saw this good furniture and, wanting to keep it, she figured, "I'll have the guy write the ticket up. Otherwise the stolen furniture will go back to the client." So she told him she was an agent, and he wrote out receipts for the furniture she had and paid for it. If she went to bed with him, she must have liked him, I suppose. But she really just wanted to get that furniture. It was greed, not love.

We have never had an agent killed. How do I explain that? Good personnel. We pick people who know how to handle themselves, and I don't mean handle their fists. We look at them very closely, and we have very close communications with them. If you went to work as a $50,000 executive in New York, you would not get checked nearly so carefully as our agents are checked.

Now it's true that we can't check whether a man can fight. But he's in trouble anyway if he's going to get into a fight. He's got to use his wits. He's got to blend in with the guys he's watching, to think the way they do. He's got to be a good actor.

Coleman and Stano are pretty big guys, but that doesn't mean a damn thing. The bigger a guy is, the greater the chance the other guy's going to use a gun on him. If he thinks he can't whip him, he'll get a gun. A little agent, whom the subject knows he can whip, is in less danger than a big guy. But on the whole, our agents don't get in that situation—they can't afford to get in that situation. We're blown on the case, if they do.

How often do we get blown? Maybe once every three or four

months. As long as you've got a volume of cases, it's bound to
happen occasionally. Often we deal with multi-thousand-dolla
thefts, so you'd think that some tough guy at some point would
try something, especially if the agent gets blown. But most
tough guys are not tough at all. Be careful of the guy who doe
not seem tough, who does not talk about how tough or rough
he is. You never know what he's going to do.

In about 1963 Encyclopaedia Britannica called us in. The
had a problem in Jersey City, so we sent an agent there,
country character who had never been east in his life. Most o
the employees there were Italian Catholics. God, how the
made fun of this guy, his accent and all. They really didn't lik
him, and they were suspicious of him as well. One day he wa
standing against a wall, and somebody pushed a big float o
books (encyclopaedias, and you know how heavy they are) a
him. This dolly on wheels, stacked high with books, came rollin
down at him, and if it had hit him, he would have been killed
It would have just mashed him right through the wall. H
jumped out in time.

When he took it good-naturedly, he was accepted. They wer
stealing Bibles, and when I made the interrogation, they admi
ted they got all their customers outside church on Sunday
They'd sell a $50 Bible for $15 to customers coming out o
church. That's just a short little story.

How come I myself have never been beaten up? Well, there
a psychological power that I have over a subject at the stag
where I first meet him—in interrogation. But that's not th
whole story. I remember one particular guy. It was an unusua
situation. The case involved a Western Auto Store. The onl
spot available in which to conduct the interrogation was a kin
of warehouse located over the store. We had to go up a fligh
of wooden stairs, and I was going to interrogate him in th
middle of the packing cases. Right in back of me was an ope
freight elevator. The grill was open, and I was standing with m

back to the open shaft. It was foolish of me. I never stopped to think of the danger involved.

As soon as I told him who I was and that we had him for stealing, he said he had never stolen a thing in his life and furthermore he was going to throw me right down that elevator shaft. And I looked around—I hadn't realized there was any elevator shaft there.

I said: "Sit down, just sit down. You're not going to do a damn thing!" This guy was 6'2", and he did sit down.

If I were to show fear at any time, I'd be gone. We've had cases where the individual would claim later that he'd signed a statement under duress. Once I was brought to court to testify. The jury looked at me and looked at the subject—he's about 5'10", 190 pounds. I'm little, 5'6", 140 pounds. Duress? Ridiculous. He didn't have a prayer with that jury.

When I interrogate a subject, I'm pretty positive in my thinking. Even if this guy's a pretty big man, he has to know that I'm not afraid of him. It's possible that my physical appearance is part of the reason for my success. The fact that I'm little and can accuse a man of stealing means that I must have proof. Otherwise I would expect him to kill me. Since I obviously don't expect that, they decide to confess instead.

I have never felt fear. And I've taken on guys I knew carried guns and knives. The client has advised me of this beforehand. Only after I've gotten a confession will I tell a subject, "You can put that gun on the table now. I knew you had it all the time." I've done that several times. I've never carried a gun in my life. Once a security man came in to an interrogation and said, "Take that knife out," and I said, "If I'd asked him in the beginning about his knife, he'd have known I was scared of him and I'd have been finished before I started." I have to take that chance.

In Chicago at the Acme Packing Company, James Jackson and Colonel Shadow both came into that little office with meat hooks sticking out of their breast pockets. Those are the famous pins they used to push the stolen beef onto the trucks, and they could have done a helluva lot more damage to my person than an ice pick. I saw those weapons in their pockets, but I just ignored them. Then when I got the confessions out of them and called in Tony Vitale, he came through the door with his eyes fastened on those meat hooks. He went right over and lifted them out of their pockets and sat there twirling them while we went on with the interrogation. But I myself never touched those meat hooks. They didn't bother me at all.

One time I interrogated a guy who had been convicted of murder and had served time for it. This was the Consolidated Laundry case. He was robbing the laundry he worked for, and he kept the merchandise in his house. I went out there with my agent to collect the merchandise. I told the guy we had him cold and that he was to get into my car because he and I were going back to the laundry. I knew he had been convicted of murder and had served time, and he knew he was about to go to jail again. But he and I just drove nonchalantly through the streets to the laundry, where he made his confession and signed the statement. What's a little murder?

The average agent working for me has never had any police training at all. I almost never hire policemen as agents. If I do we have to retrain them. Policemen are used to going after a single conviction. If they get evidence of one deal, they make a case. If they have enough to arrest the guy, they arrest him. That's no answer to the systematic stealing in America today.

The first time I had any association with an enforcement agency employee was in 1948, when I hired an ex-federal agent. This guy's integrity could not be questioned. We're still good friends. If we had to have any piece of business, he would recommend us, because he knows how we operate. But as far as being an investigator, this guy just didn't have it. He didn't know anything about investigations. The federal agency would tell him to do a little piece of work here, and somebody in New York or Baltimore would do something else, and somebody in the office in Washington would be correlating all this information and working the thing out. But actually to take a case from nothing and develop it—this he had no idea about. Most policemen or federal agents don't know anything about our kind of operation. As soon as they know a guy has stolen a tape recorder, they arrest him. Great, but what good does this do for society? What are they doing for the owners? What are they doing for the taxpayers? For the people who are paying the dough to keep them operating? They don't even ask how many tape recorders were stolen. Maybe there were $100,000 worth of tape recorders stolen. But no, they're interested only in their one little conviction. When such a case comes into court, it has no impact. The case involves nothing but one tape recorder. Juries are not inclined to convict that guy; they'll give him a suspended sentence, a pat on the wrist. The charge will be reduced to a misdemeanor. Our law enforcement officers are not trained to probe into the background of cases. They need to be taught how to do that.

Even the undercover agents that most police departments use—and some are very good or they couldn't have been operating this long—still have that same police department feeling. They're trained in police department methods, even though they may be outside informers. Because they've been working for the police so long, they think like police. I ask my guys for imagination, for ingenuity. We must make our police departments hire guys with imagination, not just people who grew up wanting to be cops. They don't have enough people like this now. Their people see police work as cut and dried, and it's not.

Many of the informants the police have are not 100 percent on their side either. So when you boil it down, how good are they?

We own a lot of equipment. We have two walkie talkies with

a seven-mile range, which is adequate. We have sixteen- and eight-millimeter movie cameras, both with zoom lenses, which can pick a subject up at two hundred yards. If we need something that requires greater power, maybe to pick up someone at five hundred yards, we rent it. Nobody owns their equipment anymore. There are so many things you might only use once that it's often better to rent.

We also have a Minox camera and a small thirty-five-millimeter camera. It's smaller than a deck of cards. In addition, we have the standard bugging devices, but you can't use them much anymore. You can't bug a conversation unless at least one party knows he's being bugged. Bugging devices are less useful today than cassette tape recorders. I can send one of my men into a room with a recording instrument on him, and he can record a conversation between him and another person because he is aware it's being done. I can record a telephone conversation as long as one party is aware it's being recorded. This is according to the federal wiretapping law passed, I believe, in 1969. They call it a wiretapping law, but it goes further than that. It applies to all transmitters. We probably have $2,000-$3,000 worth of those things which we can't use any more. We also have a debugger.

All these devices have to be simple to operate because we don't have time to train our agents in their use for a long period

The cameras we use operate well in almost any lighting condition, even inside a building. The debugging device is used to detect if a client is being bugged. It detects the impulse that any transmitter will send out.

We also have a hound-dog transmitter. It's magnetic so you can put it under the bumper of a car that you're trying to follow Some people call it a "beeper." A receiver fastens inside the car we're using, so we don't have to stay right on the tail of the car we're following. Usually we use it only in truck surveillance such as in following a delivery truck where the driver is sus pected of unloading merchandise at unauthorized places to unauthorized buyers. With the beeper we don't always have to employ visual surveillance, because if you're watching someone, he might also be watching you.

These gadgets are not used a great deal. The conditions are never perfect for them. It still takes a hell of a lot of leg work, brain work, and field experience. Of course, in an insurance case, where you have a fraudulent claimant, you have to have some kind of recorded evidence, if at all possible. In that case, we sometimes must use tapes, cameras, and bugs.

Sometimes a sequence camera is called for. Take a client whose vending machines are being robbed. It would be too costly to use an agent for surveillance ten or twelve hours a day, and he would be seen anyway if he hung around that long, so we might plant a camera in a "suggestion" box bolted to the opposite wall. It is better to plant these cameras inside the wall, but sometimes walls are solid. It takes ingenuity. We build what we need. I've even had to ask a client to build a tool shed, where we could put an agent to make his surveillance, because there was no other place to hide.

Imagination is by far the most important element in this business. The gadgets are only secondary. Gadgets can be used only under certain conditions, and even then imagination is needed to figure out how to utilize them.

We've probably spent $20,000-$25,000 on equipment, but most of it is quickly out of date and we don't really use it very much. We haven't even taken an equipment inventory in quite a while.

We have a voice-activated tape recorder worth about $800. You can plant that in a room and leave it there. In addition, we have four polygraph instruments. One is so large you have to check it as baggage when you fly, so we don't usually bring that one along. The polygraph instruments are each worth about

$1,500, not counting the supplies that go with them, and they are of course terribly delicate.

We handle cases in forty-one different categories, from A to L to R—arson to larceny to rustling of cattle (yes, that still goes on in this country)—and we work all over the United States, from coast to coast. At this moment I have an arson case in New York, a rustling case in Tennessee, and tomorrow I am sending four other agents to Los Angeles to try to stop the larceny that is going on in two hospitals there. Two of the men will work in Mount Sinai Hospital, two in Cedars of Lebanon. All four are black men. None of the agents will know one another. If they do, and if one of them gets blown, the other guy will lose his cover at the same time. So we make a point not to let two agents in the same plant know about one another.

Naturally we sometimes get reports from Agent No. 1 that Agent No. 2 has been trying to find something to steal. But we never get reports that Agent No. 2 has actually stolen. A lot of agencies condone that type of thing to give other employees the idea that their agents are crooks. I don't permit that because if I have to make an interrogation, I'm then put on the defensive. That's exactly what happened with the Howie McNeil case in the Meyer Clothing Factory. The client built up the cover story that our agent was a thief from Louisiana, and that's what made a successful interrogation impossible. Once I'm put on the defensive, I'm through. I must stay on the offensive when I'm making an interrogation. Therefore, even if that's the only way to make a case, we will not permit our agent to take any merchandise out. Our agent may help a particular subject move something to the dock, but once he gets it up to that dock, our agent won't cross that line under any circumstances.

This brings up the subject of entrapment. I've done a lot of thinking about it. There will be cynics reading this who will accuse me of entrapping the thieves I catch. I disagree. Not only do I never permit agents to actually steal something in order to prove themselves with the thieves they are trying to uncover, but I also never permit my agents to approach someone with a crooked proposition until and unless my agent knows for a fact that that person is a thief.

If my agent sees a thief steal or if the thief brags to him about stealing, then almost anything goes. My agent can ask to buy stolen goods and can buy them. He can pretend to be the worst thief in the bunch. He can carry stolen goods right up to the dock, but he cannot cross that dock and actually load stolen goods onto a truck or into a car. He can ride in the vehicle containing the stolen goods. He can't provide the vehicle in which the stolen goods are removed.

He cannot propose stealing to an employee who, as far as he knows, is honest. This, to my mind, would be entrapment, and it would also be stupid because the honest employee might denounce him on the spot, and the client would then have to fire him. Or the crooked employees might consider him a wild man or an idiot and refuse to deal with him. There is a fine line between entrapment and good tactics and my men have to know what it is, and entrapment is never permitted, and that's all I have to say on the subject. I am not a philosopher, I am a detective, and the above reads clear enough to me.

In those two Los Angeles hospitals, people are stealing drugs and a lot of other things. Linens, sheets, everything. Money and valuables are being stolen from patients' rooms. Many of the patients are wealthy, and they're losing a lot of money from billfolds and purses. That's getting to be a big thing today. At one time that never happened in hospitals; now it's common. Hospitals have to accept any warm body who will agree to work there, not only in Los Angeles, but everywhere. Consequently these people whom they hire often have criminal records; they haven't been checked out properly, they're not good people. They steal from employee lockers, from the room of a patient who's maybe unconscious or in the operating room. They steal from the hospital itself. They steal from everybody.

Some of our categories we work in constantly, and some we rarely handle. For instance, we don't do too much with politics, apart from some undercover work to see if there are any skeletons in a candidate's background. But we don't do it for free. This business makes no political judgments, no political contributions. A candidate will hire us to check into the background of his opponent, so we get the facts, and that's all we do. I don't care whether my client is the bad guy and my agents have to dig up some unsavory facts against the better candidate. If that happens, fine.

As a practical consideration, I haven't done political work in a number of years, and I never did get involved with a major candidate. I have no juicy political scandals to hide. I have stayed away from politics as deliberately as I have stayed away from divorce cases. Potential clients soon found that political cases didn't interest me, so that type of business began to go elsewhere, which is fine with me.

A number of years ago I made a decision about my business image, and I've never deviated from it. We get the facts, and that's all we do. But there is something more to it. Take insurance claims. I've never been an ambulance chaser. Even at the beginning, when I was broke, I wouldn't chase an ambulance. I'd rather work for the insurance company. I didn't want to be labeled an ambulance chaser. I've preferred the high profile. There are not many agencies who can say that. We go to great lengths during an investigation to get the information we need, but never at the price of subverting the ethics of this firm. We do things as ethically as possible, and that's the best I can say.

We handle scores of arson cases. I just met with the agent we have put into the Statler Hilton Hotel in New York. This is one of the biggest hotels in New York. It is opposite Penn Station

and gets a lot of one-night traffic. There have been nine fires of
unexplained origin there in the last few weeks. Also, somebody
has twice let all the water out of the sprinkling system. Obviously, employees are involved, but who and why?

The second night my agent was there somebody set fire to
trash in two of the rooms in the middle of the floor. Our agent's
hotel job is to collect trash from the hallways outside the rooms
the maids have just cleaned and to carry it outside into the
driveway dump bins.

So far he has no leads. He has noted that all the trash men and
elevator operators and maids are smoking on the job, which
they're not supposed to do, and that some of them don't care
where they flick their still-lighted butts. He has noted that they
all loaf on the job and think nothing of leaving their own unfin-
ished assignments for the next shift to do. He has noted silver-
ware, dishes, coffee pots and linens in the trash. Whether this
is done out of resentment against the hotel management or
whether they later reclaim this stuff from the garbage is not yet
clear.

I have recommended putting another agent in some other
part of the hotel. It's too huge a place for one man to find out
what's going on all over.

Forty-one categories.

We also handle many disability cases, particularly claims of
back injuries that are very difficult to prove. In order to prove
anything, you have to investigate the way the allegedly injured
guy moves around. You have to take pictures of his activities.
You follow a man who says he can't work, and often it turns out
that he's cheating, that he's able to do everything anybody else
can do. He drives his car, he goes to the grocery store, he can
fix his roof. We have a case right now in a town of 450 people.
The company's been paying this man workmen's compensation
for the last five years, but in that town he works as an itinerant

preacher every Sunday. We've proved he's also doing paid electrical work for people. Now it's very difficult to go into a town
of 450 people without anybody knowing you're there. And it's
also very difficult to take pictures in a town like that, so I sent
my agent out with some surveyor's tools, a tripod, a view finder,
etc., and by attaching a camera to the tripod, we have been able
to take some interesting pictures.

Disability cases can be fascinating. In Missouri recently, an
auction barn was being run by a man who had lost one leg. He
was 65 and collecting on a big policy. Officially his sons operated
the business, but it was the old man, sitting out in his big car,
who would signal to his sons the type of merchandise he wanted
put up for auction, depending on the type of customer who was
attending the auction. He was also doing all the buying. He was
running that business and we proved it. His sons were just
figureheads. We were able to contact some of his former employees, particularly maids, and they gave us the inside picture.
Any maid that went to work for him had to go to bed with him
first. A one-legged man, 65 years old. In this business you meet
all kinds of people.

Then there are the death-claims cases. People commit suicide, but the estate claims natural or accidental death and sues
for double indemnity. I had a case in New York City where a
man jumped out the twenty-third-story window of the Biltmore
Hotel. He had left home; nobody knew where he was. He had
had a light stroke the night before. A nurse was with him, and
while this nurse was changing clothes in the bathroom, he
jumped out the window. The estate claimed that he fell, that he
had wanted to get some air and had leaned over too far.

To break that case, we had to prove a strong motive for
suicide. This man lived in a town of fourteen thousand people.
I dug around that town for ten days or so. All I could come up
with was that his wife, who was going through menopause, was

inviting 18- and 19-year-old kids over to their house for cocktails and entertainment when he wasn't there. This man was disgusted with her, and every time he came back from a business trip, he would just go upstairs to his room. That's about all I could get. His financial position was good. His wife was independently wealthy, and he carried about $100,000 worth of life insurance with a $100,000 double indemnity clause for accidental death.

I ingratiated myself with the chief of police in that town. I figured he knew what it was all about, if no one else did. Finally he said: "I'm going to tell you something, but if you ever double-cross me you'd better not come into this town, because you'd be sure to get a parking ticket. And if you get any parking tickets, you're going to lie in jail for five days."

This is what the police chief told me. The dead man's brother had been visiting him, and about two o'clock in the morning the brother woke up and came downstairs and found his brother's wife with another man in a compromising position on the sofa. He woke his brother up and there was a big fight. The man caught with the wife was a prominent person in this town—a Yale graduate and a lawyer. The police were not called. The police chief never would tell me how he knew the details, but he did know them and they were facts.

The outraged husband was a sales manager for a large oak flooring company, and the next day he went to New York, had a stroke, and killed himself.

When I got that information from the police chief, I was floating on air. I drove eighty miles an hour to the attorney's office who was representing the insurance company. He said, "For God's sake, find that brother." I found him a long way away—in Tuscaloosa, Alabama. I was racking my brains. How was I going to approach this man? I was sure he'd never tell me anything. Surely he'd want to protect his brother's children.

The son was in medical school, and the daughter was graduating from high school. I never did decide what I was going to do.

I asked for him and he came downstairs. I made up a story instantly. I said, "I understand that you've been looking for a job in the lumber business and one of the people you've contacted has asked us to make an investigation. During the course of the investigation, we found out that you were involved in a fight in your brother's home. And we do know about your drinking, but we feel that's not too serious. But what about this fight?"

He said, "I felt I had to protect the honor of my brother's home," and he told me the whole story. I proceeded to sit down and write out a statement which he signed. I knew that the statement was worth nothing because it had been obtained as a result of misrepresentation, fraud, and deceit.

So I tore up the signed statement in front of his eyes and said, "This statement is of no value to me. The only way I could get you to make this statement was to tell you the story I did, but I am in fact representing five insurance companies, and we're arguing about your sister-in-law's double indemnity claim. Now if you still want to make this statement and put in that I told you whom I represent, we can do that."

He agreed. I took the statement back to the insurance companies. The attorney had also instructed me to find out about the wife, to find out if she was still running around with these young kids. So on my way back from getting the statement, I checked into a hotel in the city nearest where she lived. I very seldom sit around the lobby of a hotel, but that particular night, just as I was checking in, I asked the room clerk if there was anybody at the hotel who might be able to give me some information about this nearby small town. To my surprise he mentioned the wife's name, said that she often stayed in this hotel, and that she was there now. "I'll call her, she'll be glad to talk to you about her town."

I said, "That's not necessary."

I got washed up, had something to eat, and went to sit in the lobby with a magazine. The bellboy came over and patted my shoulder and said, "They want you at the desk." There stood the wife. I had been investigating her, but I had never seen her in my life.

She asked what my name was. I told her. She asked who I wanted to know about. I told her I was in the clothing business and was trying to find out about a store owned by a man named Miller. She said there was no proprietor by that name in her town. It was very uncomfortable for about five minutes, but I got out of that. I had a feeling she knew who I was and what I was doing there.

The next time we met was in court. She came right over and said, "How's the clothing business?"

Anyway, the case came up to trial, and we won it.

Under "M" comes missing persons, which is a big field now, what with all these young kids disappearing. If you go into a police station or sheriff's office anywhere in the United States, you'll find a whole sheet of names of young, good-looking kids on the wall.

Leakage of confidential information is another of our important categories. Companies are getting too big. In each company there are too many people who can leak valuable information to competitors. Sometimes people are employed by one company and then placed in jobs with competitors, where they serve as undercover agents for the purpose of getting information. Sometimes we're called in to find out who they are. Sometimes it's clear who they are, and it's up to us to find out who placed them in that job, why they're getting that information, and how. The best place to start looking, oddly enough, is in accounting departments, even when what is being leaked is, for instance, secret chemical data.

We just had a case in Oklahoma City. An oil broker named

Jason Mitchell was somehow obtaining confidential geological information from one of the biggest oil companies in the country. We had agents watching Mitchell and the other people involved off and on for three and a half months, and we finally broke the case just before Christmas. Mitchell was getting the information through two geologists and an auditor in the Tulsa office of the oil company. This trio had agreed that if any one of them was detected, the other two would continue to pay the ousted person his one-third interest. They were receiving their payoffs through relatives in order to avoid paying income taxes on the money. They had even agreed to discontinue their activities for the year as soon as each of them had cleared $50,000.

We deal day after day with people who are doing things they shouldn't be doing, and one of the things I've noticed is that the great majority of these people are divorced. Jason Mitchell was divorced, the auditor in question was divorced. The people I catch are usually people with little or no stability in their lives. They're not thinking about others; they're thinking about themselves. Greed gets them all, one way or another—that's the predominate factor. No question about it. We all have it, and it shows up in everything we do; but these people have more, and that's what forces them to take chances. They know they're wrong to do it. They know they're taking a chance, that they are going way out on a limb. But they nevertheless do it.

Unions don't pose too much of a problem, because an agent usually isn't eligible to join a union before he's been on a job ninety days, and we're usually out of there by then. We do not handle any labor cases. The Wagner Act, passed in the 1930's, forbids interfering with attempts by employees to organize. It is against the law to pass information to the employer about what the union may be thinking or doing or about union secrets. Nor do we handle divorce cases. There is too much good business around for me to get involved in all that messy divorce stuff. I'm not interested in whether husbands or wives are doing what they're doing.

Five or six times in my whole career I've been forced to handle a divorce case because a corporation was my client and one of the executives ordered me to investigate his wife. When I did do this kind of work, I submitted reports attesting to the fact that the two parties entered a hotel together and didn't come out again for X number of hours. I refused to break any doors down, take flash photographs, bug a room, call the sheriff, or whatever. Divorce is just too messy. I'm not so pure that I refuse to touch it for moral reasons. But I don't want to get a reputation of being that type of investigator. Divorce investigators must continually testify to salacious acts on the witness stand. This gets into the papers, and their reputations get messy. In addition, such work involves constant harassment by the clients. Such clients are terribly sensitive. All they can think of is what their spouse might be doing with someone else's spouse, right at this minute, and they call you night and day and think that the world will come to an end if you don't catch their spouse at once.

I'm sometimes asked if, after thirty-six years in this business, I have a favorite case. The answer is yes. It didn't involve murder, it didn't involve arson, it wasn't really a very serious case at all. But it is my favorite.

One day an Internal Revenue agent called me on the phone. "Mark, this is about a very close friend of mine named Lee. I have just had the painful duty of investigating his taxes. For the last three or four years he hasn't been paying any, so they sent me to investigate him. He operates a drugstore. The situation is very bad. He has no merchandise on his shelves. He's been drinking. The drug companies won't send him merchandise anymore, even c.o.d., because he doesn't have the money to pay them. To fill a prescription, he first has to go to other drugstores to get the drugs. In five days' time, his place is going to be closed by the sheriff for nonpayment of rent.

"Mark, there's a man who works for him named Buchanan. He's worked there about fifteen years. He's been bragging that he has $100,000 and that when the store closes down, he's going to take over. He told a drug salesman that he'd have that store and that he has $100,000 cash in his safe deposit box right now. This was once a prosperous drugstore. Is Buchanan responsible? If he does have that much cash, where did he get it?

"Mark, this guy Lee probably can't even pay your fee, but do me a favor and go down and see him."

So I met Mr. Lee at his home, and when the drugstore was closed that night, he took me inside. I saw an empty store. Nothing on the shelves. It's a bad situation when you can't even buy razor blades or toothbrushes. So I agreed to do a job of investigation for $100. I figured I'd never get this money, but I'd work on a percentage of what we recovered, if we recovered anything. Lee was honest. He said he didn't have $100, but just for the sake of argument, we'd make a contract. Together we made a record of what little merchandise there was in the store, because I intended to send shoppers in to check up on the clerk, Buchanan.

In the next several days we made thirteen purchases in that drugstore. Each night Lee examined the retail register tape, and the buys that we made were not recorded. None of my three or four shoppers watched to see if the clerk rang up the sale. He would have recorded the sale if he had known he was being watched. We would make two purchases, ten or fifteen minutes apart, and Lee would ring up a "no sale" before them and after them so we could find where they should be on the tape. The store was not busy, and it was easy to determine that our buys were not recorded.

The following Monday I questioned Buchanan. I called to him

from across the street and talked to him in the lobby of the old Nicholas Hotel. My client was with me. We told Buchanan that we had made purchases from him and that they had not been recorded.

He said, "You go to hell."

I said, "If that's the case, then I'm going down to your bank right now and I'm going to check your lock-box."

I knew I could not get into his lock-box, but he was in shock and wasn't thinking straight. He thought I could do it. He said, "I'll just go down with you."

I said, "That's great."

So the client, Buchanan, and I walked down the street to the Phillips National Bank. The bank cashier got out the key and opened the little room. We went in and Buchanan opened the box, which contained tons of money. He opened it because he was still in shock. People who are guilty do a lot of things they wouldn't normally do. He had plain envelopes marked "forty $50 bills" or "twenty $100 bills." He had every denomination. He started counting the envelopes, and then he realized for the first time that he didn't have to show me anything. But I went over to the president of the bank and said: "I am putting you on notice as of now not to touch that box. If anybody comes in there and takes money out, you're allowing this at your own risk. In ten minutes I'm going to have an order tying up this box."

This druggist Lee was a member of the volunteer fire department. He was very well liked in town. Everybody knew he had to have some money to stay alive.

He and I went right over to the county attorney's office. The county attorney and the sheriff drew up some legal-looking papers so that the bank could not let that money go. The papers had no legal value whatsoever. Even the banker knew it, but since the order came from the county attorney's office and the sheriff had delivered it, he put a seal on Buchanan's lock-box. We were only stalling for time. If the case came to a hearing before a judge, the judge would throw it out.

Within thirty minutes after that box was sealed, Buchanan had looked me up. He said, "My attorney is Ralph Tucker. He wants to see you."

I went to see his lawyer. I knew him and had done some work for him. He said, "The papers that were served on the bank don't mean anything."

I said: "I know that and you know that. Meantime, we need the money and you know we need it. I've got a case. I can have your guy arrested, and I intend to do it. I've nine counts of misdemeanor against him. He can get a year and $500 fine on each count. He'll serve time—there's no question about it. Lee is popular in this town."

The lawyer said, "Let me see what I can work out."

Monday and Tuesday passed. No word. Wednesday, Thursday, still no word. I decided to move. I went to the police and told them to lock Buchanan up, to arrest him on nine counts of embezzlement.

We arrested him. The next day Buchanan's lawyer called me. Would we take $5,000? Lee had to have money. Buchanan had stolen much more than $5,000, but I couldn't prove it. And $5,000 was a fortune to Lee at this point.

They brought in the $5,000, and we dropped the case. Then a strange thing happened. When it hit the papers that Buchanan had been arrested for embezzlement, people who owed Lee money, some for years, started paying him. All the drug wholesalers to whom he owed $1,000 or $1,200 each, got together on the telephone to see what they could do for him. They decided they would each give him merchandise so that he could operate. They suspended his over-account, and they gave him credit. They put in about $5,000 worth of merchandise. There were about nine of them. He and his wife went to work;

within a month they had the place painted, and within a year they had it air-conditioned. Two years later they sold it and paid everybody all that they owed. Then they moved to Virginia, and I haven't heard from them since.

4. Carter, Tennessee: Stolen Furniture

•

Why does an executive steal from himself, and how?

May 14

There is a firm called S&K Kitchenettes in Carter, Tennessee. It's a big firm, part of a Chicago-based conglomerate. S&K sells kitchenette sets to Grants, to J. C. Penney, to the major chain stores all across the country.

Three Saturdays in a row, before dawn, prior to the arrival of the regular work force, a truck has been observed being loaded at the S&K Kitchenette docks. Finally word got back to Chicago, and Chicago called us. The fourth Saturday was May 1. We had an agent there all night to see whether that truck would show up again, and if so, where it would head.

This is our agent's report for that day.

1 A.M. Agent established surveillance, taking up position just outside the fence to the north of the plant.

Surveillance was continuous with no activity noted until 4:10 A.M. At this time, lights were turned on in the office area of the plant. The lights were left on for a few minutes, then turned off again.

5 A.M. The lights are again turned on. Agent is unable to see anyone inside the plant.

5:20 A.M. At this time, truck entered the plant area and drove to the loading docks on the south side of the plant. From agent's point of surveillance, agent is unable to tell what is occurring.

6:20 A.M. Truck left the plant and agent noticed that the truck bore Tennessee tag number PM 1985. The driver of the truck was a white male, heavily built, with light hair and complexion. The truck drove to Memphis via Highway 51 and stopped at a storage-type building on Morgan Lane.

The man entered the building and reappeared in the company of a middle-aged woman a few minutes later and opened the rear doors of the truck. The truck was full, mostly of cardboard cartons of the chair and table variety. Agent also noticed uncrated chairs and tables.

7:45 A.M. The driver began to unload the truck and was joined shortly by two black men. The unloading took until approximately 8:30 A.M. Agent estimated eighty kitchenette sets were unloaded from the truck and brought into the storage area.

Agent returned to this area later in the day and noticed that the portion of the building in which the furniture was loaded is accessible by two doors, which are padlocked. All windows are either painted over or boarded up. One end of the building is used by Jones Garage, and agent could see that no merchandise was inside the garage. The other end of the building is used by a florist, and agent could see that no merchandise was stored here.

Further investigation of the Tennessee plant revealed that it would have been impossible for the truck which entered the plant on the morning of May 1 to get into the plant without help; that they have a guard and three dogs that are vicious; that the truck apparently entered the plant without any problems.

Agent talked confidentially to man working at the plant who stated that there has been quite a bit of dissension. It was common knowledge that a woman who worked in the office had been for a long time embezzling large sums of money and had been caught.

The client, Mr. Jackson, who was from Chicago, met with us several days later and discussed what we ought to do about the situation.

S&K Kitchenettes was formed twenty years ago by three Gould cousins. About three years ago they sold their operation to a major hotel chain, who operated it as a subsidiary but never made money and so sold it to the conglomerate Chicago firm.

Two of the Gould cousins still operate this company for the conglomerate. When they owned the business outright, they ran it without regard to records. Because of the looseness of the operation, it was probably very easy to put money directly into their pockets to escape taxes. Now that they don't own the business outright, they are apparently doing more than just cheating the government out of taxes. When the Goulds sold S&K to the hotel chain, they reportedly taped up empty boxes to cover an inventory shortage of $30,000 to $40,000. A man by the name of Tony Smeriglio was in charge of inventory control at the time. It is thought that he is related to Cy Gould.

Some weeks ago another employee, Mrs. May Cascoe, was caught stealing. Somebody came in and bought some kitchenette sets worth $200 or $300, and she turned in about $25. When she was dismissed—they had an airtight case against her —the president, Cy Gould, pretended to be indignant and very surprised that this trusted woman was stealing.

Investigation has shown that May Cascoe is now working for Gould's cousin, Ray, who has started another operation similar to S&K Kitchenettes. Investigation has also shown that Mrs. Cascoe used to be Cy Gould's girlfriend, and it seems clear that, until she had to be fired, she was helping the Goulds loot the company. Apparently the Gould brothers are stealing from each other, too. A lovely case.

Only Cy Gould and the youngest of the cousins, Gene Gould, are left in the business. When they sold their company, they each got about $1 million in stock, plus long-term contracts, to go on running the company. Cy is president and gets $50,000 per year. Gene gets $30,000; he keeps a desk there but rarely shows up or works. They're millionaires, but they're stealing.

We went on with the investigation. We had one agent working inside the plant, and we had two outside agents following the Goulds and Mrs. Cascoe. After two weeks, their reports totaled forty-seven single-spaced pages.

May Cascoe is 42 years old, 5'8", dark-complexioned with frosted blond hair. She dresses expensively, drives a late-model car. We have the details of the divorce she got a few years ago. Another man was named as correspondent, not one of the Goulds.

Cy Gould's sons, Billy and George, are both on the payroll of S&K Kitchenettes. Billy is a pretty good worker when he is there, which isn't too often. George draws fifteen hours pay— at $2 per hour—each week, whether he works or not. He seems to come in about once a week. When he's there he either loafs or sleeps. In other words, Cy Gould doesn't have to pay these kids an allowance. The company pays it.

One day the agent assigned to Cy Gould parked near his house and photographed it. He also made a diagram of the layout. We don't know where this investigation is going or whether or not we need such information. At 12:30 A.M. that same night, our agent came back to Gould's house for the purpose of establishing the makes and numbers of the cars parked there. He waited until they seemed to be asleep inside, then walked up to the cars and turned on a flashlight.

Our agents also checked out the tag number of the truck which had been making those dawn pickups and found that it belonged to Waldo Monroe. We began following Monroe. On May 7, watching from inside a fruit market across the street, we saw the May 1 furniture being reloaded into a rented U-Haul truck. We followed this truck out past the golf course to the Red Barn Auction, where the kitchenette sets were unloaded. After the truck was gone, we talked to the saleslady, who said the sets would be auctioned off on Sunday, two days later, for $30 to $35 each. They're worth $100 retail.

We were present at the Sunday auction, but Monroe withdrew the kitchenette sets at the last moment. After he left the scene, our agents approached the saleslady, who remarked that Monroe's other items had not sold well, so he had decided to withdraw the kitchenette sets to wait for a better day.

We kept digging. We found out that S&K produces about twenty truckloads of kitchenette sets per week. Each truck contains either sixty-five wooden kitchenette sets or one-hundred aluminum ones, which means that one stolen truckload per week amounts to 5 percent of the total production of the factory. I don't know what the profit margin of the factory is, but I doubt it's any more than 5 percent, and it is probably less, which explains why both the hotel chain and the Chicago conglomerate lost money while owning this factory.

We picked up facts and also rumors. A man named Cox, controller of the factory, told us that Cy Gould, Gene Gould, Ray Gould, and Mrs. Cascoe had a long-standing "game." The "game" was to see who could steal the most from the company. According to Cox, the game started when the Goulds owned the company outright and continued during the ownerships by the hotel chain and the Chicago conglomerate.

We interviewed a man named Fuller, who had worked for S&K for a year, who stated that one of the Goulds carried a gun and had once fired the gun in the factory to get attention. The Goulds ruled the plant with an iron hand, and no one knew anything that the Goulds did not want him to know. Mrs. Cascoe, who had been Cy Gould's secretary for about twenty years, had complete access to all files and records. According to Fuller, no records were kept of any kitchenette sets listed as damaged merchandise or of returns or cancellations. These

kinds of merchandise went out of the plant to salvage and sec-
ondhand shops and auctions, as directed by Mrs. Cascoe. Fuller
believed Mrs. Cascoe then shared the proceeds with Cy Gould.

Fuller named an ex-secretary, Sally Jo Jenks, who had quit her
job because Cy Gould insisted that as a condition of employment she go to bed with him. Mrs. Fuller, who was present
during our interview and who had once worked for S&K Kitchenettes, said that this happened quite often with female employees there, but that she herself had never been proposi-
tioned by Cy Gould.

We began picking up rumors about kickbacks. The owner of
the truck company who has the contract with S&K Kitchenettes gives a new Cadillac each year to both Cy and Gene
Gould. Cy Gould is also supposed to get some kind of kickback
from Denman & Denman, the metal supplier for S&K Kitchenettes.

We found a man named Dan Bester who quit S&K a month
ago because of "company graft and policies." He said bluntly:
"The Goulds are stealing that company blind." He said the
Goulds owned pieces of various furniture stores, outlets and
salvages, but he could not name any of them specifically.

The reports go on and on, forty-seven pages already. Mostly
the reports are of surveillance, agents sitting outside places,
waiting for something to happen; agents tailing cars that don't
go anywhere significant; agents circling the block on which one
of the subjects lives. Here's an entry for May 13: "7:40 A.M.
Subject came out of the house in blue pajamas and house slip-
pers, took a newspaper out of the mailbox and stood in the
driveway reading it for six minutes. 7:46 A.M.: A little girl, approximately four years old, in pink nightgown, left the house
and took subject back into the house." Very touching.

We're going to have to move fast now. The problem is going
to be to get the Goulds out of that plant on some pretext so that

I can interrogate some of the other people, especially this black man, Hedley, who we have learned is the one who came to work in the middle of the night to load those trucks. Also the night watchman.

But how do you get the men out of the plant who, in effect, own the plant? And why would the Goulds, who are millionaires, steal? Especially Cy Gould, who apparently is a really talented executive and salesman? Here's a guy who's making $50,000. He's living well, he's got a family, he's happily married. But he was stealing from himself even before he sold his company. He was stealing because he was trying to evade taxes. He got in the habit of stealing. When he started to do that, first thing you know he's got a couple of girls he's playing around with. This is a fact. He's playing around with a couple of girls. He does not want to deprive his family of all the good things of life. He doesn't want to cut down on his insurance or spend his capital, so he's picking up that extra money to take care of these women.

Uncle Sam has taught a lot of these people to steal. If they didn't have to pay taxes, they wouldn't have thought of being crooks. Sometimes we've tried to sell our service to companies only to have the company president refuse to admit there was stealing going on there at all. He was afraid any investigation would uncover some of the things that he himself was doing. Sometimes we come across a guy who'll admit stealing, but he'll say, "I learned how to steal from the boss. I stole for him. Why shouldn't I get something for myself?" That's a common thing.

Which brings me back to the Goulds. How are we going to get them out of that plant so I can interrogate these other people and open up this case? The Chicago conglomerate is not going to put up much longer with unpaid-for merchandise leaving that factory by the truckload.

May 30

The Chicago people flew in here two days ago to discuss their case. How was I going to break it? They said they thought we ought to break it now. They didn't see any point in continuing the investigation.

I said: "I'd like to go down there and talk to this fellow Hedley first, the black man who loaded this merchandise onto the truck on May 1. He had to know something about this. If you could get Mr. Cy Gould away from the business on some suitable pretext, that would give me time to talk to Hedley and also to a man named Tom Beede. Mr. Beede is your warehouse superintendent. He was told about these dawn shipments and knew when they were going to occur. At the start of this investigation we didn't know why or how he could know in advance, but we know now."

The Chicago conglomerate is one of this country's industrial giants. They were listed in the top three hundred by *Fortune*. Their men began to discuss with me breaking the case at once —never mind Hedley and Beede—and I began to agree with them, not because I wanted to agree with them, but because I liked the somewhat unusual method they wanted to follow. I thought it was sound. We would use our Memphis office and bring Cy Gould in. We would tell him that we've got reason to believe there's a lot of theft going on, that there's a possibility that he could be involved, and that we want to know what he wants to do about it. And I told Mr. Dowd, who headed the client delegation: "He's going to tell you that he wants to help you get to the bottom of this. That's exactly what he's going to do."

Dowd called Mr. Hyman in Pittsburgh but found that he was in Atlanta, and Hyman flew in here without even an extra shirt.

Everybody came to my office at 8:30 yesterday morning. Mr. Dowd, Mr. Jackson, and Mr. Hyman represented the company. The three of them brought Cy Gould to my office. They sat on my sofa. On the left was Mr. Dowd; on the right, Mr. Jackson. Cy Gould was sitting in the chair facing the door. Mr. Hyman was facing him. I was sitting on another chair off to one side.

Cy Gould is kind of a dapper Dan individual, dark hair with sideburns, dresses nicely, Miami Beach type of guy. He's about 40. He's the salesman of the firm, the type of guy who goes to New York and gets the contracts. He runs the business. Gene Gould, who was not present, is supposed to be in charge of the warehouse, but actually he doesn't do anything. The company has hired some other men to run the warehouse.

I had told Mr. Hyman I was going to let him take the lead on this interrogation and I would get into the act when I thought it was appropriate, but now Mr. Hyman started talking to Cy Gould in a very negative tone: Hyman thinks this did happen, maybe it did, did Gould know anything about it? This line of questioning is nonsensical. Hyman said, "Well, didn't some merchandise leave the plant at 5 A.M.?"

Cy Gould said, "That's impossible." Then he said, "That could only be one person, my cousin." Then he stopped, realizing he had made a mistake.

He said, "Impossible. We need to find out about the five o'clock operation. There's no way that could happen. We would know about it."

I said, "Well, it did happen, we know it happened, we saw it happen, we can prove it, there's no question about it. Do you want to help us, or don't you?"

He said, "I definitely do."

I said: "Are you sure you're not involved? Tell me how Mrs. Cascoe stole all this money all these years, which we haven't tried to prove at all. It was proven on one occasion only, and that's when you fired her. You're also involved in another company that makes tables, a new company run by your cousin, Ray, called the Wearever Manufacturing Company, which is in competition with S&K Kitchenettes. It has a capitalization of only $20,000, and this same woman is working over there. You're vice-president, you must know something about this situation. You wouldn't hire a known crook in a brand new business that has got a capitalization of only $20,000. Somebody could hurt you fast."

He said he was trying to help his cousin. Ray wanted to start this business. They weren't going to make tables, they were going to make lamps, and this Mrs. Cascoe knew the business and wouldn't have access to any money.

This type of nonsense went on for quite a while until I said, "We're going to call this black man, Hedley, up here." I left the room and gave orders to bring Hedley up to our office. Hedley was not to be told why. Hedley is on the payroll; we can ask him to go anywhere. A few minutes later the plant called back and said, "I'm sorry, but I can't bring him up there. Hedley is washing Mr. Gene Gould's car."

I said, "I don't give a damn whose car he's washing. This is an order. Get him and tell him this takes priority; we need him up at this office." Hedley was washing the car at the plant in Carter, Tennessee, which is a good distance away from Memphis.

Roy Hedley has been a trusted, really a very trusted, employee. He's a black man who's been working there a long time. If Ray or Cy or Gene Gould said "flip," he'd flip. If they say "Wash my car," that would come before anything else. Hedley would do anything they wanted. And the reason is that if he ever needed any money or had a problem, all he had to do was ask and they'd take care of it for him. Really, he is of the old-time southern school; he may not get a hell of a lot of money, but when the chips are down he is always taken care of. Anyway, Hedley was a man the Goulds could depend on, and Gene and Cy knew that.

When Hedley came in, I took him into one of my other offices. Mr. Hyman came in too. I started talking to Hedley as I usually do, asking him his name and his age. I wanted to get a little background on him. But Mr. Hyman cut right in and said, "I want to know if on May 1 you were involved in merchandise leaving the plant at 5 A.M.?"

"Definitely not," said Mr. Hedley.

I said, "It's not a question of whether you were involved. We know you were involved. We actually saw it." And then I detailed to him how we watched the plant all night. I read to him from the report, which detailed all that happened on May 1. I read it piece by piece, verse by verse.

He said, "Yes, I do know about that."

I said, "I have a carton here. On May 3, 1971, Monday morning, one of our agents retrieved this carton. It's marked S&K Kitchenettes, Inc., in yellow printing. According to this other label, this merchandise was being shipped to Frank's Furniture, Jasper, Alabama. This is a carton that was put on that truck."

He said, "Yes, I remember that. The merchandise had been sent back from Jasper, Alabama, because one of the chairs had a little knick in it. The whole six of them came back."

"That is some of the stuff you loaded onto Mr. Monroe's truck?"

"That's right."

I said, "I just want to know one thing. Who instructed you to put that furniture on that truck? You usually come to work at seven o'clock. You were down there at 4:30 in the morning. You turned the lights on, you turned them off, to signal the truck, you waited and waited until this truck came in. Who instructed you?"

He said, "I can't say."

I said, "Well, you're going to say it. I'm going down from the top and I want a yes or no answer. Was it Cy Gould?"

"No. Not Mr. Cy."

"Was it Gene Gould?"

Hedley said nothing.

Hyman said, "Was it?"

Hedley wouldn't answer.

I said, "He's not going to protect you. We're going to talk to him. He won't be able to protect anybody."

Hedley said, "Yes, it was Mr. Gene."

That was the first real break. Hyman suddenly saw proof that the top people were really involved.

We proceeded to get the details from Hedley. Hedley said this had been going on since January 1970—a year and a half. Mrs. Cascoe had told Monroe, the trucker, to call Hedley at home at night. Monroe was to give Hedley two or three days to accumulate enough merchandise to put in the area. Once it was ready, Hedley would come to work at 4 or 5 A.M., instead of at 7:30, and load the truck. The previous night Mrs. Cascoe would make up a bill of lading or an invoice. Of course later that bill of lading or invoice would be destroyed. Monroe would go in later and pay Mrs. Cascoe cash. Each time Hedley would load the truck he would get a $5 tip, or they would give him a shirt or something.

When Mrs. Cascoe was fired six or seven weeks ago, Gene Gould told Hedley, "Now I'll call you and tell you when to come down here at five in the morning." Hedley got nothing extra beyond this tip. He did not even punch the time clock at 5 A.M., and I asked him why.

He said, "Well, Mr. Gene has done a lot of things for me and I'm just paying back some favors."

By this time it was about twelve o'clock. We had talked to Hedley about twenty minutes, and now we dictated the report for him to sign. All this time we were walking back and forth between offices, keeping Cy Gould informed, which was his right as president of that division of the company. He had a right to know what was going on. When Hedley's statement was ready, we had Cy read that statement. He didn't have his own glasses; I had to lend him mine. He glanced at it and said, "I understand."

I said, "You couldn't have read a three-page statement in one minute. If you were the fastest speed reader in the world, you couldn't do it."

He said, "Well, I already know what's in it," which indicated that he knew well enough what had been going on.

I said to him, "I want you to read it word for word. It's your obligation now as president of the company to call Gene on the telephone and tell him to come up to this office. I know it would be painful to have to do this to an employee who had been working for you for twenty years. With a cousin and a partner, somebody you have worked with all your life, it must be a very painful operation. It's tough to do. I realize how tough it is, but it's something you have to face up to. This is Judgment Day, and you are going to have to do it."

But finally Mr. Dowd, who's really the boss of all these guys, called Gene and asked him to come to my office immediately. Gene hesitated. He apparently knew something was going on, because his man Hedley had been gone all morning. And Mr. Cox, his controller, had been gone a while too, because he had brought Hedley up here. Anybody with a little intelligence would know that something unusual was happening. So then Cy got on the phone and told Gene that he wanted him up at our office. Gene has always been the obedient brother, so he started up.

The trip would take him about forty-five minutes, so we decided to get something to eat. I gave Hedley a couple of dollars. He said he didn't need it, but I gave it to him anyway. I said

"I want you to go down the street to get something to eat and then come back as soon as you can."

Mr. Dowd, Mr. Jackson, Mr. Hyman, Cy Gould, and I went to Jim's Restaurant about half a block down the street from my place. We all sat there and talked—we didn't talk about this case particularly, just about generalities. Cy had no trouble getting his food down. He ate normally in every respect, even though you could tell he was drained. Cy was wearing beautiful black pants, thin, tight pants, very expensive, and nice shoes. He wore a beautiful yellow shirt with a pin stripe. He wore a yellow tie and a yellow blazer. I said to him, "Well, that blazer must have cost you about $100," and he said, "No, $150."

Nobody drank or smoked. Nobody drinks when I'm making interrogations.

We got back to the office about 12:45, and about four minutes later Gene Gould walked in. Gene is separated from his wife right now. He lives by himself like a hermit.

Cy decided that he did not want to be present when we were talking to Gene. Gene sat in the same chair in which Cy had sat earlier in the interrogation. The only ones who remained in the room were Mr. Hyman, Mr. Jackson, and I. Mr. Dowd and Cy went into our conference room.

We talked at great length to Gene about that Saturday morning shipment. He absolutely would not say anything. The May 1 shipment was the only one we actually saw, even though we knew there were at least three others before that. But there was no question about May 1; we had it cold as ice. The whole investigation was predicated on that information. Anyway, Gene denied it ever happened, even after we told him Hedley had already told us the story.

Mr. Hyman called me out of the room and said, "We're in bad shape. We're no better off than we were this morning. This is terrible. How do I know that Hedley told the truth?"

I said, "Don't worry about it. I've already arranged for Hedley to be polygraphed."

So I went back into the office and told Gene that Hedley was being polygraphed and that in five minutes I would give him the results of that test. And then Hyman called me out again and said, "This is bad."

I said, "Will you please relax? You're a lawyer, and lawyers are the poorest investigators in the world. I know you're bright and you're my client, but I'm telling you that lawyers are not good investigators. Let me work this out. Give me a little chance, give me five or ten minutes more—the man's only been here five or ten minutes. It'll work out. You know damn well that Gene is involved. You were willing to talk to Cy for a couple of hours because you weren't sure. But now that you know Gene is involved you want it settled instantly."

I went into my polygraph examiner's office, let him read Hedley's statement, and told him exactly what I wanted checked. He polygraphed Hedley on a very short chart, to determine whether the statement he had given was true or false. The statement checked out true and correct on all counts.

Now I told Mr. Hyman, Mr. Jackson, and Gene Gould to wait a few minutes, and I went into the conference room where Cy Gould was waiting with Mr. Dowd.

I said, "Cy, you're in a hell of a mess. Your cousin will not say a word. There's only one person who can handle this thing, and that's you. If we don't get this resolved right now, if Gene doesn't tell us the truth, these Chicago guys are prepared to make an extensive investigation. That means more money for my company, more profit, more business, because they're not going to stop at anything. You can't tell who will get involved —Internal Revenue and a lot of other agencies. I know damn well you've got the information. Hedley was telling the truth— you read the polygraph report. I think we can prosecute Gene right now. We saw the merchandise coming out of that plant.

We saw Hedley help load the merchandise. We saw where it was delivered. We saw Monroe take the merchandise. We got an identification of some of the merchandise that Hedley has already signed. He identifies it as merchandise he loaded. We've got your brother cold. He's your brother. If you had any sense, you'd straighten him out. I'm giving you five minutes. I don't give a damn which route you go. For God's sake, if you have any sense at all, take advantage of it."

Then I said, "I'm going to bring Gene into the conference room, and I'm going to let the two of you talk this over. I'll be back in five minutes, and by that time I expect you to say that he's going to tell me the truth."

I brought Gene into the conference room and left him there with Cy. Five minutes later the door opened, and Cy said, "Gene will tell you the whole story."

Gene then told me exactly what Hedley had said was the truth. So I brought him back into my office and said, "Tell these other gentlemen, the officials of the company, the true facts." He now admitted that he had been involved about four times in the last six weeks, about $200 each time, which amounted to about $700 or $800 in stolen merchandise. We typed up the statement, and he signed it. We also typed up a letter of resignation from his $30,000-a-year contract, and he signed that, too. This contract had two and a half more years to run.

Gene kept saying, "How stupid can I get? How dumb can I be, to lose a $30,000-a-year job for $800—and I didn't need the money."

Finally I said: "You were just doing what you had been doing all your life. You couldn't get out of the habit. It didn't make any difference whether you were worth 10 cents or $10 million. It was a habit. It was all you've known how to do all your life. On the side you sell seconds, old merchandise, junk merchandise, and a few pieces of good merchandise that you throw in; you've been doing that all your life." I didn't say anything about Cy's knowing about it or being part of it.

The net result was that everybody left. Mr. Dowd had to get back to Pittsburgh for one day before returning to Mississippi for the shake-up of the S&K organization, which was scheduled for tomorrow. He left first, and at 4:40 we told Gene he could go and he did. Cy then said he would take Mr. Jackson and Mr. Hyman to the airport.

Today they closed down the plant at 3:30 P.M. The whole organization is closed down pending reorganization. Everybody is to call in tomorrow, Friday, to find out if he still has a job.

It developed that Cy Gould was not involved. I'm not sure of that myself, but the clients want to believe he is not involved, and they are going to leave him with his $50,000-a-year salary.

It was in the company's best interest to cut if off the way they did. They preserved their organization. They kept their president, who is a very competent man and who is scared enough now not to try anything for a while.

I couldn't say anything. You do what the client wants.

I guess that sounds like a weak ending to this case. We get a confession from one man—he admits to having stolen only $800 —and we stop.

I could have interrogated Mrs. Cascoe. I could have interrogated the trucker, Monroe. We could have taken this whole mess back to three years ago when the Goulds sold out to the hotel chain. A good deal more than $800 worth of merchandise disappeared in that time. But the client is happier this way. They saved $75,000 on Mr. Gene's contract alone; they no longer have to pay him for a job he isn't doing anyway. They have stopped a big leak. The reorganization allows them to put controls on Cy for the first time. Oh, they're happy, all right.

I'm not too happy though. There is so much stealing going on in this country, and most of the people doing it never get caught. The few investigations that do get done get cut off before they reveal much more than the surface.

You almost have to conclude that it pays to steal. If that's true, then the stealing is never going to stop. I hate to think what America is going to be like twenty years from now.

5. Cincinnati:
The Polygraph Is Infallible
•

Is one of our six salespersons stealing?

June 4

Today we broke the Rand Boutique case, and we did it with the polygraph alone. Rand's is a lady's shop in downtown Cincinnati, and the owner complained that $30,000 worth of merchandise had disappeared in the last few months. Where had it gone? What could I do to save his business?

Ten weeks ago I put one of my female agents in there as a salesgirl. She is a crack girl, Gail Richards. She has worked for me for over two years, and I have placed her in stores and factories in Dallas, Omaha, Birmingham. In Philadelphia she worked as a packer for a manufacturer of ladies' clothes and developed the information that helped me break that case. She eats, sleeps, and breathes undercover work. She even married one of our agents. When this happened, one of them had to go, for I didn't want both of them working for me. It's too complicated. Obviously, they'd always be comparing notes on cases. The two of them together would know too much and talk too much. In addition, I would be responsible for settling any disputes between them. I would not have the freedom of assigning one of them to one city and the other elsewhere. So I put it to them. One of them had to find another job. The one who stayed with me was Gail.

Then I put her on the Rand Boutique case. She's good, she's trustworthy, but in ten weeks she came up with absolutely nothing, at a cost to the client of over $2,000 in fees.

I could see that the client was getting more and more nervous. Every time I picked up the phone, he was on it. What was he getting for his money? When were we going to find out who was robbing him? Rand Boutique is part of a chain but does only about $150,000 worth of business a year. You can imagine what that $30,000 loss represents. They have a total of six employees in there, and one of them, Gail, is ours.

I decided to move in with the polygraph. In order to be polygraphed, each employee must give the company and our agency a complete release. Those employees who are not guilty often don't mind being polygraphed, because when it is explained to them that a loss has occurred, they would rather have themselves cleared. However, sometimes even innocent employees will resist the polygraph, so I advised the client to announce that the bonding company required it for insurance purposes. This was true, and saying it usually calms down the employees, one of whom, in this case, was almost certainly a thief. My only job was to find out which one. When I am on a case, I am single-minded. The employees of that shop had to be polygraphed.

At this point I thought I knew who the thief was—John Grubert, the manager. Grubert is a tall man of about 60. He sits at the cash register, I was told, and the salesclerks bring him the tickets to be rung up. He handles all the customers' money. He can come and go any time he wants to. He does the buying; he has the keys to the place. His wife, Mrs. Grubert, worked there too. I never saw her, but they told me she wore real fancy clothes.

When the client went into the store and told them they would all have to be polygraphed, Grubert flushed and got very nervous. He said that because of his age and heart condition, he shouldn't have to go through something like this. The client replied that he wanted everybody polygraphed.

After the client had left the store, Grubert called over all the other employees, including Gail (who nobody knew was my agent), and tried to convince them that the polygraph was illegal, unreliable, and that their constitutional rights were being violated. He wanted everyone to refuse to take the test. He argued that if they all refused, then no one would be fired. But he couldn't get them to agree.

I don't know whether the client threatened to fire anyone or not. Clients are not supposed to do this, but sometimes they do.

Every day or so, after the shop was closed and the shades pulled down over the doors, Grubert would call the sales force together. The polygraph was unconstitutional, he told them, and it was also humiliating, especially to himself as manager.

I scheduled the examinations over several days. Grubert was supposed to go first, but he broke the appointment. We examined several of the salesgirls, and they were all clean. We made another appointment for Grubert, and he claimed to be sick and did not come to work at all that day. Today his vacation was supposed to start, so it was the last day to nail him before he would be out of reach for several weeks, receiving full pay for every day of that time.

About noon he called to break the appointment again. He was too sick to come over, he said. The client told him he had better keep the appointment. Grubert then said there was too much work at the store and he wanted to clean it all up before leaving on vacation. He didn't have time to be polygraphed today. Couldn't it wait until after his vacation?

The client stated that he would like to get everything cleared up today, if possible. "Be here at three o'clock," he said, and hung up.

While waiting, I went over a few things with the client. I do not do half-baked investigations. When I come in on a case, I want to know everything. In recent months that shop had been burglarized twice. I had gone over the police reports and the inventories before and after both burglaries. It appeared from these papers that Grubert had tried to minimize the first break-in, possibly because he was embarrassed and felt responsible. Of course, if he had been stealing, you'd think he'd maximize the quantity of missing merchandise to cover what he had taken himself.

I paused again and considered this fact. There was something wrong there, but it wasn't clear what.

After the second burglary, the client made a claim for $1,800 worth of stolen merchandise. The inventory was completed a few days later, and this amount proved to be about right.

"You're certain of these inventories?" I asked the client again.

"Yes. Those burglaries have nothing to do with the $30,000 shortage."

"You've checked all the other paperwork?"

"Yes. The missing $30,000 has nothing to do with incorrect figuring."

There are many more ways for a manager to steal than for a simple clerk. I doubted that any of the other employees could have stolen so much so quickly, and in any case, all of them had by now passed the polygraph tests except Mr. and Mrs. Grubert.

"Do you think it's Grubert?" the client asked.

"If all you have told me is accurate, there is no other possibility."

And in my mind, Grubert was already guilty. It was him or nobody. The polygraph would merely verify this.

"Does the polygraph ever make a mistake?" the client asked.

"The polygraph itself is infallible," I told him. "But the instrument is only as good as the examiner, who must be an expert."

"I suspect Grubert of receiving kickbacks from salesmen, too."

So we sat there, waiting for Grubert to appear.

There is no such thing as a lie detector. The polygraph is an emotion detector. It records physiological changes which take place in the body: blood pressure, respiratory pattern, and galvanic skin response. This last item refers to the measurement of excess perspiration in the fingertips or palm, for under normal circumstances, people don't perspire significantly in those places. But they do when they lie, and the electrodes attached to the fingertips pick it up.

Then there is a tube which goes around the area we breathe from. Men are lazy breathers—they usually breathe from the belly, from below the waist, so the tube goes around the midsection. Women usually breathe from above the waist, so the tube goes under the bust. This tube measures any change in breathing pattern. Sudden intake of breath, that sort of thing.

The third instrument measures blood pressure; it's a cardiograph machine. Although we're not looking for the same thing the heart specialist is, sometimes we do find, when checking for the truth, that people have heart damage that they didn't know about.

A licensed polygraph examiner takes the same anatomy and physiology course that a medical student does. The course is taught by an M.D. There are four accredited polygraph schools. One is associated with the armed forces and is located at Fort Gordon. The other three are civilian schools associated with universities. There's Gormac, which is affiliated with Los Angeles State College; Keeler, which is part of the University of Chicago; and Backster School of Lie Detection, which is part of

New York State University. There are about five thousand examiners practicing today.

The lie detection course takes about six weeks. Candidates usually must have a college degree.

The whole idea in administering the polygraph is to exonerate people. An ethical examiner will not try to put subjects on the spot. He will try to get them to relax so he won't get any extraneous reaction.

I always say to the person who's going to be tested, "For God's sake, if you're involved in this thing, don't take the test. If you're not, go ahead and take it."

An ethical examiner—and those who work for me are ethical —won't ask any questions which he hasn't reviewed beforehand. If the subject is not involved, even the hot questions don't bother him. If he is involved, he gets psyched up about the hot questions that he knows are coming, and it shows on the graphs.

Sometimes there will be a reaction which is not completely explainable. We had such a case the other morning. The person polygraphed answered the questions truthfully. She was a decent sort of a person and didn't want to drag in two others who were involved. The graph showed she was not involved herself, but the specific reactions indicated she had knowledge.

Of course, if a wife is involved, as was thought to be the case with Grubert, that's an even closer situation.

Lie detection has been going on since at least 250 B.C. They have a history of it in woodcarvings at Northwestern University in Chicago. There's one story of ancient lie detection where a donkey with soot on his tail was put in a darkened room. The suspects were to go in the room and pull the donkey by the tail. If the donkey brayed when his tail was pulled, that man was guilty. The idea was that the guilty man would not touch the donkey's tail; therefore, there would be no soot on his hands.

There's another story about a Greek physician in 350 B.C.

who felt the pulse of a prince who was rumored to be in love with the young queen whom the prince's father had recently married. He had been losing weight and languishing because of what seemed to be a dreadful disease. In talking with the prince of the young queen's virtues, and at the same time feeling his pulse, the physician could feel a sudden tumult. The physician informed the king that his son was not sick but was trying to conceal a consuming passion for the queen.

We could use one of the lie detector's three components, but we always use all three. Sometimes a person's response to one of the components is not very strong. That's why we need the other two components.

About 200,000 polygraph examinations are given in the United States each year.

The key to lie detection is formulation of questions and sharp interpretation. If you create the right emotional stimuli for the yes and no answers, that individual who is being polygraphed will react strongly. If your questions are weak, the reaction will be weak.

The formulation of questions depends on semantics. The examiner might say to a college professor whom we were questioning about a missing $500, "Did you wrongfully take this money?" He'd never say that to a truck driver. Instead he might say, "Did you steal this money?" If he said "wrongfully take," the truck driver would know what was meant but wouldn't react much. Or if he said "steal" to the college professor, the man might not react much because he isn't a thief, he wrongfully took something.

Your questions can be weak because of a poor examiner or poor case study.

We don't ask personal questions with the polygraph—for example, questions about marital fidelity—although unethical examiners sometimes do. If we did use the polygraph for detecting marital infidelity, something like the following could happen, and it could be ethical. Suppose a wife came to us and said her husband was fooling around with Jane Doe. We would then ask the man, after hooking him up to the lie detector, if he was fooling around with Jane Doe. If he wasn't and he trusted the examiner, he would come out clean. Even if he was fooling around with someone else, if he believed that the examiner was only going to ask him questions pertaining to Jane Doe, he would come out clean.

The polygraph only indicates *conscious* truth or falsehood. It can't verify questions such as Do you love your mother? That's an opinion question. The polygraph can't rate opinions.

If it is used ethically, if it is asked to measure yes or no responses to programmed questions, then it is infallible, and it can be read infallibly by a skilled examiner. Thus a skilled examiner can in fact play God. He can get inside another man's head and know what only that man should know. It is a direct invasion of the privacy of the human mind, and I don't like it at all, but it is a tool which I use because it catches crooks. There are cases where we could be swimming around in lies for days. The polygraph lets us cut through all that in seconds. I measure a small invasion of privacy against the crime I see all around me, and crime wins, and I use the polygraph.

Unscrupulous and incompetent examiners are ruining the polygraph as an investigative tool, and it's possible that use of the instrument could eventually be outlawed by Congress.

More and more it is being used in preemployment testing. It can tell the employer if the prospective employee has ever been arrested or if he has filled in all the questionnaires accurately. My men do use it that way, and they use it ethically. But I have heard of examiners who throw in sneak questions and who then "measure" the responses, who lie to the subject about the graphs, and before you know it the subjects are confessing to youthful homosexual experiences or to breaking into cigarette machines as teenagers. Some subjects not only don't get the job they are applying for, they get fired from the one they already have. Marriages break up. Subjects are forced to leave town.

And the unscrupulous examiners destroy the reputation of an impersonal instrument. Already the polygraph has been disavowed by the FBI. Meanwhile the CIA uses it widely. It has no legal value in court, but the National Security Agency and the U.S. Civil Service Commission use it. Many unions are succeeding in having its use outlawed with regard to any testing of their members. The New York City Police Department wants to use it in corruption investigations but so far is being blocked by the policemen's union there. However, the Los Angeles and Chicago Police Departments and many other police departments use it routinely in corruption cases.

The instrument itself is infallible, and in work like mine it can be invaluable. I'm not interested in suggesting ways to weed out unscrupulous and incompetent examiners. That's not my job. My job is to catch thieves and to break cases, and, although my feelings about it are certainly mixed, I'll go on using the polygraph to help me do it.

At three o'clock Grubert came through the client's door. He was so scared he was trembling. He answered a few questions from the client. He didn't look any of us in the eye. The client didn't shake hands with him, and neither did I. The client led him into another office and left him there with my examiner and the portable polygraph instrument, which was already set up on the desk, with all its tubes and wires and antennae spread out in several directions. The examiner closed the door. The subject, Grubert, was now alone with the examiner and the instrument.

The client and I sat down to wait.

"How long will it take?"

"It all depends."

"Grubert sure was nervous."

"Yes, he was."

"Do you think he did it?"

"We'll soon know."

"Is the instrument really infallible?"

"Yes."

He went on asking questions like this that I was in no mood to answer. He asked me how many cases I had solved by using the polygraph. I told him they were countless. Had I ever known it to fail, he asked. I mumbled something. I do not usually tell my clients anything about my methods of working. I don't want them to know anything more than they have to.

Nonetheless, I was remembering a case in St. Louis where the polygraph figured prominently—Bertram's Furniture Factory. Big shortages. Mr. Bertram called me, and we agreed that I would place an agent inside the warehouse. The warehouse superintendent was advised because that was the only way an extra man could be put to work there.

The agent had been with me a long time. He was dependable, stable. But after four or five days the warehouse superintendent, whose name was Elvis Swayne, started calling Mr. Bertram, saying: "This detective is terrible. Everybody in the warehouse knows he's a detective."

I flew to St. Louis, met with Mr. Bertram, and advised him that we had better start watching this Elvis Swayne. "You've got a problem," I told him. He didn't believe me, of course.

He said, "It's funny you say that. We got an anonymous call today to watch Elvis Swayne. It must be just a coincidence."

I later learned that Bertram thought I was the one who had made the anonymous call. He thought I was a phony.

I said, "Let our man stay in there until the end of the month. We'll see what he picks up during the inventory period."

In this way our man was able to pick up leads against some of the truck drivers. Nothing firm. A joke here, a remark there suggested to him that two of the truck drivers were dishonest.

After we pulled our man out, Mr. Bertram told Elvis Swayne, "You were right, we spent money for nothing. That guy was no good. Everybody in the plant knew he was a detective."

I had told Mr. Bertram: "Put him to sleep, let him go to sleep, everything is fine."

We lulled Elvis Swayne to sleep, then sent another man, a good outside investigator, to St. Louis. He hung around bars where the two truck drivers went on their routes. He stayed there two or three weeks. He didn't do anything except hang around those bars listening and buying drinks.

Finally he told one of the crooked truck drivers that he'd like to get a mattress if it was cheap enough. They went through a tricky deal. The driver wanted to know where the agent's car was. He wanted the keys to the agent's car. He was suspicious of our man. But greed gets them all. The truckers even called him a detective to his face. They nicknamed him Captain Cop. But they still went through with the deal because they wanted the money.

There were several drivers involved now. Once they took him back in the head in one of these tough bars and threatened to cut him up. They then promised to get him some stuff, but they didn't do anything that day. They spent the day looking in the rear view mirror thinking they were going to be followed because they felt sure he was a detective and they had promised to sell him stolen goods. Fortunately, we didn't have them followed that day. If we had, it would have been all over. Any time a man's looking for a guy to tail him, he's going to spot him.

Anyway, our man did buy a mattress. We were able to determine that it was a Bertram mattress. Then we rented an apartment on their route. Our agent told them he had moved in there and wanted to fill that place up. So then they started bringing him merchandise by the case load. That apartment was soon loaded with merchandise. We spent a couple of thousand dollars for furniture.

As soon as the case looked solid, I flew to St. Louis to interrogate the drivers.

At the last minute, Mr. Bertram wouldn't permit me to make the interrogation. His lawyers said no. They weren't sure of me; they wanted the police to handle it. So we all went out to the St. Louis County Police Department and talked to a captain there. He ordered one driver and one helper arrested. Presently they were brought into the station house in handcuffs.

The police wouldn't let me question them. This often happens. When you call in the police department, they want to handle it. So two city detectives questioned the two guys, and they confessed only to what they had had in their truck when arrested, nothing else. The police interrogator asked, "What about Elvis Swayne?"

"No, sir."

So the captain said, "I'm going to have you polygraphed."

The truckmen agreed. They were pretty cool by now. They were sent into a room to be polygraphed, and the report came back negative. Elvis Swayne was not involved. We had to accept it, but I didn't believe it.

These police departments are interested in getting a big case. If you bring them a case that's not big, they're not impressed.

The captain said to me, "What kind of crap have you brought in here? This is lousy; it's not worth a damn."

So I said, "Let's call Elvis Swayne down here. These truckmen work for him, and Swayne knows they're in trouble. He's going to leave that warehouse. When he comes in here, let me have him for three or four minutes, that's all. You can have him for the rest of the day, but let me have him for the first three or four minutes."

We had two company vice-presidents there. They had no authority. They were just stooges, but they were vice-presidents. They had to call Mr. Bertram, the boss, and get permission for me to interrogate Swayne for three minutes.

I met Elvis Swayne alone. The office door closed. I said, "These two truckers told about you. They confessed everything. We know just how bad you're involved. It's been a long time. Just give me an idea how much you've gotten."

His face had gone white. He said, "I haven't gotten any more than $15,000." Right off the bat. So I walked out. It wasn't more than a minute. I said to the police captain, "Mr. Swayne wants to talk to you. He's admitted about $15,000." And I'll never forget the expression of those two vice-presidents—they were shocked, just completely overwhelmed by this one-minute operation.

I said, "I'll tell you what you do now, Captain." I was a little bossy then. I said, "You talk to Elvis Swayne and develop the other people involved and I'll be back in about an hour."

He said, "Where are you going?"

I said, "I've got a little idea that I want to work out. If it's successful, I'll tell you. If it isn't, I won't say anything about it."

I called the two vice-presidents and said, "We've got work to do." We got in the car and drove out to that warehouse, and we opened Swayne's desk. We found so much evidence that it was unbelievable. He had records of unrecorded merchandise. He had two little notebooks that constituted his own personal accounts receivable record. He had sold company merchandise to all the employees in the warehouse at cut-rate prices and had kept the money. He had sold stuff on the installment plan. If men didn't want to come to work that day, they'd call Elvis Swayne to punch their time card so that they'd get paid anyway, and they paid him $10 for that. Everything was down in those two little books. The two truckers we had just arrested, although the polygraph showed that they did not know Elvis Swayne, were right in those memorandum books too, which proves that the way in which the examiner interprets information is what counts.

It's just like your doctor can read your god-damned electrocardiogram, which is really the same as the polygraph, not a bit of difference, it's just one of the components used by a polygraph instrument—your doctor can read it wrong. Lots of guys can get it and drop dead on the way out of the office.

A polygraph examiner has to know what he's doing, or the instrument has no value whatsoever.

From my experience, I have found that only about one in ten polygraph examiners actually knows what he's doing and that many clients accept the word of the examiner as fact, when instead the examiner may have misread the graph.

To me, there is no substitute for interrogation. If an individual admits to a good interrogator what the facts are, you can depend on it, assuming the interrogation is not made under duress. These days I do interrogations in three minutes or less. Certainly there cannot be much duress in that short period of time.

Polygraph is an investigative aid, but for many years I have usually been able to accomplish my purposes without the polygraph, and in the few cases where I have found it an investigative aid, I would rather have done without it.

Elsewhere in the security industry too many people depend on polygraph exclusively.

I believe that Senator Sam J. Ervin of North Carolina was correct in submitting a bill to prohibit both the federal government and private industry from using the machine to screen job applicants. He also stated that the lie detector or polygraph is "one of the most pernicious of all the pseudo-scientifics of the twentieth-century soothsayers."

Now, that's an exaggeration. There is no doubt that the polygraph in the hands of a capable examiner can be of extreme help in investigations, but it must be used sparingly and with great care and with great skill, and interrogation is a far superior tool.

About ten minutes had now gone by. The client was smoking.

He kept putting out cigarettes after about three puffs. In the next room sat the manager, Grubert, 60 years old, tall and thin, wearing a shabby suit, sweating heavily. And across the desk from him sat my examiner, explaining the procedure of the polygraph as it is used by examiners who work for me.

"I'm only going to ask you a few questions," the examiner told him. "I want you to try to relax. There will be no surprises. I am now going to tell you what the questions will be. I will write them down for you. Here they are: (1) Is your first name Lewis? (2) Do you live in Ohio? (3) Have you stolen any cash or merchandise from Rand Boutique during the last twelve months? (4) Do you smoke? (5) Do you drink coffee? (6) Have you ever told a lie? (7) Did you answer all the questions truthfully?"

During the first two control questions, the examiner would adjust the recording graphs to correspond to the degree of the subject's nervousness. The third was the hot question, and the graphs would jump if Grubert lied. The reason the examiner also asks "Have you ever told a lie?" is because it is guaranteed to get a response. Otherwise the individual might not be responding at all, while the examiner assumed from his lack of response that he was telling the truth. So you ask, "Have you ever told a lie?" Everyone has lied. The subject considers some whoppers he has told, and there is an emotional response which the instrument records. He then answers either yes or no. Either way, the instrument records a severe reaction.

The examiner kept up a stream of chatter as he tightened the tube around Grubert's chest, attached the electrodes to his fingertips, and wound the blood pressure device around the manager's upper arm. The examiner always talks to subjects constantly in order to relax them as much as possible and also in order to determine what kind of man he's dealing with.

In this case he learned that Grubert originally came from Philadelphia. The same outfit that owns Rand Boutique also owns a chain of jewelry stores across the country, and Grubert had worked for many years in one of these stores in Philadelphia before being ordered to move to Ohio. He had been in Cincinnati for four years. He said that his wife was very unhappy and that he hates Cincinnati also, but that the company won't let him move back to Philadelphia. My examiner learned that Grubert, even though he is the manager, is paid a salary of only $9,000 a year.

The examiner now went over the questions with Grubert again, then began to ask them formally.

He came to the third question: "Have you stolen any cash or merchandise from Rand Boutique during the last twelve months?"

Grubert swallowed hard, then said, "No."

The examiner continued to watch the graph. His expression did not change. He went on to the next question.

After the seventh question, Grubert asked anxiously, "How did I do?"

The examiner said, "You did fine, don't worry."

Grubert said: "Don't you think that if I had stolen that money I'd be better dressed than this, that I'd have a car, any kind of car?"

After unhooking Grubert from the instrument, the examiner came into the next office where I was waiting with the client and said: "He's clean. He did not steal that merchandise."

I looked at the client, and I felt pretty disgusted with him. "We've now polygraphed everybody except Mrs. Grubert," I said. "We also did a ten-week undercover investigation that turned up nothing."

"It must be Mrs. Grubert," said the client.

"If Mrs. Grubert were guilty, it would have shown on her husband's polygraph," I said. "He would have had a stronger reaction. Not as strong as if he were stealing himself, but strong. My agent will polygraph her too before he leaves here today, but I guarantee that she is not involved."

The client said: "But we're missing $30,000 worth of merchandise."

"If the polygraph tells me that all of your salespeople are clean, then they are clean," I said. "That merchandise is lost in your bookkeeping somewhere, or else more was stolen in those two burglaries than you thought. Those are the two places I'd look for it. I'll phone you in two days." And I walked out of there. Case closed.

As I said previously, the main job of the polygraph is to exonerate a suspect. This is the one job it does superlatively. Even though it had just done this job, I left that place in a bad mood. I deal with real life, not detective novels, so the missing merchandise did not fall through a trapdoor, did not vanish due to some secret chemical, was not stolen by the client himself because that client is a rich businessman who had just flown in there that week himself. No, it would turn up in the bookkeeping, as I had said.

You may think my job is a constant series of triumphs, but it's not. Because of incompetent bookkeeping, incompetent management, I had been forced to put that old man, Grubert, through a needless ordeal, and now I would be forced to send the client a stiff bill for work that never should have been ordered. Furthermore, I had invested a good deal of my own thought and energy in this case. My job is to catch thieves and break cases, and here there was no case—there never had been —so I went down in the elevator and out onto the street feeling frustrated and annoyed.

6. Waco, Texas:
More Stolen Pants

●

The punk with seventy pairs of pants in his closet

June 25

I'm sitting in the coffee shop in the Dallas airport waiting for the 10:30 P.M. flight to Waco, where tomorrow morning I expect to break a case in one of the National Clothing Company factories there. We won't get to Waco until long after midnight, and some of the people I want to interrogate tomorrow are working on the night shift. They will get off at 7 A.M., which is also when the day shift comes on, so that's the hour I have decided to begin interrogation.

This will be a short night's sleep for me.

The company is losing an awful lot of pants. The loss may amount to as much as $100,000.

My agent on this job is a fellow named James Sterling. He's white. All the thieves involved here are white except one. Sterling's been working there since April 3, almost three months. He's working as a maintenance man inside the plant and has reported that people wear merchandise out of the plant, put pants inside their clothes, and load boxes of clothing onto the trash truck for a short trip to the dump.

This is another example, a perfect example, of a company that is too lax. The company is inviting, almost allowing, stealing. They're not putting in enough controls, and they're not paying workers enough. Perhaps they're paying all they can; still, today's workers can't live on any $2 per hour, even in Waco. So they take merchandise to augment their salaries. They either sell it, wear it, or give it away to friends. Giving it away makes them feel like big shots, builds up their ego. It's one of the major motives for stealing in factories today.

The people I will interrogate tomorrow probably have closets full of merchandise at home. The company, once I have the signed confessions in hand, may send the police out with warrants to recover the merchandise, and they may have the thieves arrested. More firms than ever before seem to want to take this route, thinking it deters the thieves still left in their plants. I don't agree. I don't think prosecuting someone and putting him in jail is any deterrent to crime by others, any more than I think electrocuting murderers prevents murders.

The only deterrent would be to put in more controls. Stealing is far too easy. The company, for instance, had a guard service on duty at night but not in the daytime. Now what's the point of that? The guards slow down the stealing on one shift out of three. Even on that one shift, I'm told, they don't check the outgoing trucks.

If the interrogation goes well tomorrow morning, I'll probably take on as many of these thieves as possible. But usually the more people you interrogate, the wiser they get, so you don't do as well with the later ones. So it's best to stop after five or six.

I'm hoping to get a lead on someone who wasn't even spotted during the investigation. So far there is no sign of a wholesaler or major fence. What was seen here by Agent Sterling was stealing by about twenty guys, a couple of pairs each a day. That means Sterling has seen about two hundred or three hundred pairs of pants stolen each week. That's $1,500 a week lost to the company. There were probably many more people stealing whom we know nothing about. After all, our man wasn't working on every shift, and he was working in only one department.

National Clothing has several plants in the Waco area. It's an important industry in town, and it's not unionized. I'll go into their No. 5 plant tomorrow at 7 A.M. and I'll be able to take my first prospect at 7:15. It won't take longer than that to set things up. I'll keep Sterling, the agent, in another room as a backup, but I probably won't have to confront anyone with him. I don't usually have to, but you never know how a case is going to turn out. You might deal with a very tough guy and come out smelling like a rose, whereas with an easy guy you might fail. You never know. This case doesn't appear to be too difficult, though.

Sterling, our agent, is a very clean, well-brought-up guy. He's clean as a hound's tooth. He's a good maintenance man. He's a good man all around. He's leaving us though. He met a girl here in Waco on this job, and married her. Now he wants to settle down. Very clean, very gentle. He's never given us one minute's trouble. Never borrowed any money. He's 26 years old.

Here are some of the facts that Sterling developed:

1. John Bogardus—drinks on the job. Wears styles to work that are not yet on the market. Steals pants nearly every night.

2. Bill Lester—gave the agent a blue jean vest and Size 31 brushed jeans. Put a box containing sixteen pairs of jeans in a garbage truck.

3. Haney—stole a vest from the box. Wearing products not on the market.

4. Gerald—seen four times taking pants out under his clothes.

The agent was never able to make a purchase. The subjects were always giving him clothes for free.

We have done work for this company before. We had a case in their Florence, Kentucky, plant. The man in charge at the plant gave the wrong person a truck containing $18,000 worth of merchandise which was supposed to be going to Indiana. A simple truck hijack. The FBI came in and couldn't find a thing, so the company finally called us.

We had a crack agent doing the undercover work on this case. If the men he was watching had found out, they would have killed him. One night I remember waiting for him back at the hotel until 4 A.M. He was in a bar with the suspects and wouldn't leave them. I was so worried I sent another agent to the bar to get him. The agent signaled to this crack agent to meet him in the men's room. He told him that I wanted him out of there because it was too dangerous. He didn't pay any attention. He didn't get in until four in the morning. He was, however, an extraordinarily good man. Now he's manager of the Guardsmark offices in Atlanta. He finally did find out who had hijacked that merchandise.

The company brought the FBI back into the case, and they wanted to do the interrogation. I told them I would do it, but they had to do it themselves. Eventually they convicted about five guys. I felt I would have got more than that. At any rate, the company made a big claim for the shortage.

The first day he was on this case in Texas, Sterling saw that the women employees were making far too many trips to the parking lot, to their cars, and that every single girl carried a big purse which could have held several pairs of pants. Within a couple of days, Sterling was watching guys stuff new pants into their trousers and then calmly pull the shirttails over the slight bulge. All this was taking place in full view of the women who worked in the plant.

Sterling never did get friendly with any of the women, and at this moment there is no hard evidence that any of them are actually involved in any of the wholesale stealing—beyond the big handbags and the many trips to the parking lot.

After being in there one month, Sterling saw someone named

Gerald Boot steal a whole box of pants. Boot remarked that he had to do this to make up for the loss of a day's pay when they were laid off due to lack of business.

One night Sterling found two guys playing with the master electrical switch, trying to figure how to turn off the lights to the parking area so they could take pants out to their cars. They played with the various switches but couldn't find the right one.

Sterling found a guy named Rob Wilson who stole jeans by wrapping them around his calves and pulling up his socks over them to hold them in place. When Sterling asked him about his thefts, this man claimed to be the lowest man on the stealing chart.

One day Harold Burns told the agent to tell Lester to bring all the merchandise stashed in the garbage truck to Harold's garage. Harold told the agent he was bringing out some new girls' jeans with black and red stripes and that he had also stolen a new large gold-colored fire extinguisher. Pretty soon Sterling got so familiar with all this that he could tell when a man was walking out with pants just by looking at him. He said a man would have a "straight-shouldered look," and of course his shirt would be outside his pants.

There's going to be a new plant soon with a conveyor-belt system. Everybody is talking to Sterling about trying to steal everything possible before the new plant opens.

As I read on in this report, the references to the women become more and more numerous. One day toward the end of July there was a purse check. The women were all called into the cafeteria, and when the word got out that their purses were about to be checked, there was a mad rush for the restrooms. There was a problem that day with the toilets getting stopped up with jeans.

One day the agent talked to a man named Haney. Haney

claimed he didn't have very many jeans or slacks at home. Yet he claimed that he had stolen about five hundred pairs of pants since working for the company but that he had given most of them away.

In his report, Sterling wrote that a man named Bill Lester had a lot of stolen pants at home and should break easily. His wife was pregnant, and he'd been talking about how much he needed money since she quit work. They have a late model car, a new $850 motorcycle, an apartment that's definitely above middle class. He's living much higher than his paycheck. I'll take Lester on at 7:15 A.M. tomorrow morning. It's now shortly after midnight, and I can see the lights of Waco below.

June 26
7:30 A.M.

First of all, we couldn't find a door that was open to get into the plant. The sun was just coming up over the plain. One shift was coming out the side door as our taxi drove up, and we finally had to stop them and ask how to get into the executive offices to see Mr. Fischer, the client. He was inside but just hadn't thought to have someone at the door to bring us to him.

Anyway, a lot of the people quitting work for the day saw these strangers drive up with suitcases and gear, and the chances are that our appearance has already caused talk inside. This is Waco, Texas, and how often do people like us bang on the doors at 6:45 in the morning? There are people in that plant who are guilty and who think they see a cop every time they meet a new face in the hallway. At any rate, being seen was the first blow to the surprise that is so essential to a successful interrogation.

Next, Fischer went out into the factory looking for Bill Lester, whom I wanted to take first. Fischer couldn't find him and still can't. He went wandering through the plant looking for him and finally asked another guy to look with him. They are both nosing around in there now. Do you think all this activity is going to pass unnoticed?

I had asked Fischer to hold over three men from the night shift, and he did do this. He has them loading a truck somewhere. By now they are probably also highly suspicious and busy constructing alibis. I was going to take Lester first, our strongest case, then the three from the night shift, and then the rest of the day thieves.

Now I've changed my mind. Our surprise factor is either already blown, or else it will be blown very quickly once two or three men disappear from that floor. We can't afford to fool with the night men as well. I've decided to sacrifice those night men and just interrogate day men. This is not a union plant. Fischer can fire those night men any time he wants. He doesn't need a confession—he knows they're guilty from Sterling's reports.

He needs confessions from a large enough group to get his money back from the bonding company, and my way is the best way to get the multiple confessions we have promised. But where is Fischer? Where is the first subject, Lester?

I keep saying that surprise is vital and that's true, but sometimes you lose it, and you have to get by without it.

There was a case involving $100,000 worth of sheets and towels which had disappeared from five Little Rock hotels. We didn't know whether they were being stolen at the laundry that handled all five hotels or at the hotels themselves. We began following suspects. We watched men dump bundles of sheets and towels outside of town somewhere, and we retrieved all this stuff. The case was going well.

Suddenly one of my agents called me at three o'clock in the morning. He had just picked up a guy whose trunk was crammed full of sheets and towels. I reprimanded him for flushing the case at that time and said, "Please, bring him down to our office in the Wallace Building. Handle him gently. Let him know he's not under arrest."

I quickly got dressed and went to our office at 3:15 in the morning. I didn't want to wake the president of the company at that hour, and the other suspects hadn't come to work yet, so I had to sit there and talk to this thief about nothing. I didn't discuss the case, didn't even mention the case. I just talked to him and told him I was going to have to wait for Mr. Burke, the president.

I was afraid that if I started the interrogation and he admitted his involvement, and then we had to wait two or three hours until the executive came, the thief would then repudiate his confession. In the meantime he was sweating for three hours. He knew he was caught, and he was trying to think up some kind of alibi.

About six o'clock in the morning, after sitting there for two and a half hours talking about nothing, I called Mr. Burke, who ordered the suspects called in early, and about 6:30 in the morning we started making interrogations.

We had no element of surprise whatsoever. It was tough. I started talking to several of these guys, and I eventually ran out of room to operate in the executive end of this place. I finally got one of them in the bathroom, and I broke him right there. When I got through, I had about $200,000 worth of confessions. We wrapped that up about noon that day. But that was a long day—from three o'clock in the morning until noon—all because we didn't have surprise on our side.

Here comes Mr. Fischer now with a youth who I suppose must be Bill Lester, our first subject. As I shake hands with Lester, I'll give him a big smile.

7:45 A.M.

LIPMAN: Sit down. What's your name?

LESTER: Bill Lester.

LIPMAN: How old are you, Bill?

LESTER: Twenty-one.

LIPMAN: You married?

LESTER: Yes, sir.

LIPMAN: Any children?

LESTER: We're expecting in September, sir.

LIPMAN: How long have you been married?

LESTER: Three years come October.

LIPMAN: Where do you live, Bill?

LESTER: At 8488 Church Street.

LIPMAN: How long you been working here?

LESTER: Since November last year, sir.

LIPMAN: What's your job?

LESTER: I'm a shipping clerk.

LIPMAN: How much education do you have?

LESTER: I have a high school diploma.

LIPMAN: How much are you making here?

LESTER: $2.30 an hour.

LIPMAN: Does your wife work?

LESTER: No, sir.

LIPMAN: Do you have any other relatives working here?

LESTER: No, sir.

(So I stared at him. I bit off the end of my cigar, still staring at him.)

LIPMAN: This is the most important conversation you're going to have in your life. I'm a private investigator. Do you know what that is? A private detective. We know about the stealing that's been going on in this plant, and we know what you've been doing. We've called you in here to give you the benefit of a private conversation. We know you've been getting stuff out, and we know how long you've been doing it. We know you've been putting it on Blandon's truck. We've got a whole record of this thing. If you want to straighten it out, fine. If you don't, we'll handle it another way.

(He didn't say anything. His mouth may have dropped open a little.)

LIPMAN: You've been working here since November. We know it's been going on since February of this year. Did you start right away or did you wait until February?

LESTER: February.

LIPMAN: Now we know what you've been taking, but just tell me. How many pairs do you average a week?

LESTER: About two pairs.

LIPMAN: What do you do with them?

LESTER: I wear them. I've given a few away.

LIPMAN: How many do you have at home?

LESTER: Not that many.

LIPMAN: Have you sold any?

LESTER: No, sir.

LIPMAN: Now tell me how you do it. I already know, but tell me anyway.

LESTER: I put 'em in a box and then in the truck.

LIPMAN: The truck goes to the dump. And then you pick them up there?

LESTER: No, sir. He delivers them to me. I don't want to get into that.

LIPMAN: You'd better get into it.

LESTER: The driver . . .

LIPMAN: Blandon?

LESTER: Yes, sir.

LIPMAN: I've got his name, see? You're not telling me anything I don't already know. Does he do that for everybody?

LESTER: I don't know.

LIPMAN: He comes to your house?

LESTER: Blandon never comes to my house. He puts the jeans in my car, or I go to his house.

LIPMAN: What's the most you've taken in one day?

LESTER: In one day? A couple pairs.

LIPMAN: Have you ever taken as many as ten out in one day? Just think about that now.

LESTER: Not for myself.

LIPMAN: Now wait a minute. That makes no difference. That's not the point. What's the most you ever took out in any one day?

LESTER: Fifteen.

LIPMAN: Now what did you do with the fifteen?

LESTER: I only got two pairs.

LIPMAN: Did you sell any of them?

LESTER: No, sir.

LIPMAN: Did you give them away?

LESTER: I don't know what happened to them.

LIPMAN: What you do you mean you don't know?

LESTER: I put two pairs in the box.

LIPMAN: Is that the way you always do it? A number of you put clothing in a box to be put on the truck and then delivered to you?

LESTER: May I ask you one question? Who else do you know about?

LIPMAN: I'm not going to tell you that. You're going to tell me. I just want a yes or no answer. Yes if they were involved, no if they weren't. Bogardus?

LESTER: Yes, sir.

LIPMAN: To what extent is he involved?

LESTER: I don't know. I don't have much contact with him.

LIPMAN: How do you know about him then?

LESTER: People tell me.

LIPMAN: Who told you?

LESTER: Uh, Robbie, I don't know his last name.

LIPMAN: Has he taken some?

LESTER: Yes, sir.

LIPMAN: What about Jerry Boot?

LESTER: No, as far as I know.

LIPMAN: How about Harold Burns?

LESTER: As far as I know he hasn't.

LIPMAN: How about Martin Collins?

LESTER: Yes, sir.

LIPMAN: How many did he get?

LESTER: A few.

LIPMAN: Floyd?

LESTER: Yes, sir.

LIPMAN: And Brian?

LESTER: I don't know a whole lot about him.

LIPMAN: How about Maxie? He's a loader, I believe.

LESTER: No, I don't think so. To be honest, I can't say.

LIPMAN: Gerald?

LESTER: Well, I know he took some a long time ago. He told me about it.

LIPMAN: Did he tell you the extent of it?

LESTER: No, sir. How about Jim Sterling? How about him?

LIPMAN: What about him?

LESTER: I gave him a couple of pairs.

LIPMAN: I'm making a note of that. How many pairs do you have at your house right now?

7:50 A.M.

LIPMAN: Come in. Good to see you. Sit down and get comfortable while I ask you some questions. First of all, what's your name?

HEARN: Robert Hearn.

LIPMAN: How old are you, Robert?

HEARN: Nineteen years old.

LIPMAN: Are you single or married?

HEARN: I'm single.

LIPMAN: How long have you been working here?

HEARN: Approximately three months.

LIPMAN: Where do you live?

HEARN: 28–44 Highland Park Lane.

LIPMAN: How much education do you have?

HEARN: I graduated from high school.

LIPMAN: Who do you live with?

HEARN: Parents.

LIPMAN: How much do you make an hour?

HEARN: $2.15 an hour.

LIPMAN: I'm a private investigator. (He stared at me and then began to giggle.)

LIPMAN: We know everybody's been stealing here, including you, you understand? We know about it. What's the most you ever took?

HEARN: I'd say maybe a pair.

LIPMAN: Have you ever put any on the truck?

HEARN: No.

LIPMAN: Where do you work?

HEARN: I used to work back on the docks.

LIPMAN: What do you do now?

HEARN: I'm a ticket writer.

LIPMAN: I'm going to be candid with you.

HEARN: Will I be prosecuted?

LIPMAN: No.

HEARN: I took five pairs. A pair of jeans, a pair of vests.

LIPMAN: Lester said he had four pairs for you at his house. Did he or didn't he?

HEARN: No, sir.

LIPMAN: Three of these pairs were 34/30 and one pair was 32/30, right? How did he get them out?

HEARN: By putting them in a box and then on the truck.

LIPMAN: How about Gar Stacker? Do you know anything about him taking anything out for his wife or himself?

HEARN: No, sir, I don't know anything about him.

(I shouted, then slammed down my fist.)

LIPMAN: Let's get this straight.

HEARN: I want to talk about it, but you don't have to get riled. Let me think about it a minute. Lester got a pair of pants for me the first time, a Size 40. The second time Lester put them in a box. I never even did touch them. Now the third time, that was a week and a half ago, we took three pairs. And that's the only time.

LIPMAN: Just how many pairs did you take altogether?

HEARN: At the most, at the most, eight or nine.

LIPMAN: Is everybody stealing?

HEARN: A lot of them. That's just the way people are. You can't be perfectly honest.

LIPMAN: Have you no compunction about stealing? Doesn't it bother you?

HEARN: I wouldn't steal from a store, but when you see a mountain of pants, I know it's not right, but it doesn't seem wrong to take some. Everybody does it.

8:05 A.M.

LIPMAN: Now, Mr. Blandon, you've been working for the company over a year. How many pairs of pants do you think you've gotten in these fifteen months? Do you think you averaged about a couple of pairs a week?

BLANDON: No, sir, nowhere near that. I got about sixty pairs at home.

LIPMAN: What do you do with them?

BLANDON: Well, I wear a pair and then I wear another pair.

LIPMAN: You've just got a good selection. You must have taken out an average of twenty pairs a week.

BLANDON: No, sir.

LIPMAN: You took pants out for all those others on your trash truck. Think about it.

BLANDON: Yes, sir.

LIPMAN: Why did you do it? Do you think it's stealing?

BLANDON: Yes, sir.

LIPMAN: Did you think it was coming to you, that it was owed you?

BLANDON: No, sir.

LIPMAN: Did anybody ever ask you to move any case merchandise? To steal it?

BLANDON: Yes, sir.

LIPMAN: Well, who was it?

BLANDON: It was Jerry Baumgartner. He wanted to take case merchandise, but I told him I wasn't going to mess with that. He worked in the cutting room, and then he got mad and quit.

LIPMAN: How many pairs are we talking about that you're responsible for? About two or three hundred pairs, aren't we?

BLANDON: I didn't think it was that many.

LIPMAN: Well, you got thirty pairs out when you were working for the warehouse. There were five people you were getting merchandise out for there. And you've been working here in this plant 13 weeks, times 5 that's 65, times 2, that's 130 right there.

BLANDON: Not that many.

LIPMAN: Well, they've all said they've been getting out a couple pairs a week and you're the guy who gets them out for them. Now tell us your method of operation. I'll give you a little start. They get a box and they accumulate merchandise in it, and then they take that box down to the shipping dock, right? And how do they get it on the truck?

BLANDON: On the trash truck.

LIPMAN: And then you take the trash to the dump, right? Then you get that box out of there, and they come to your house to get the pants. Does your wife say anything about all that traffic coming back and forth? Do you bring those boxes in the house? And they pay you some money for doing it. Oh, yes, they do. You've been paid some money for that trash.

BLANDON: No.

LIPMAN: But they've been giving you merchandise.

BLANDON: Well, pants.

LIPMAN: Haven't you thrown some of these pants away? Worn them out or given them away?

BLANDON: About ten pairs I gave away.

LIPMAN: So that makes about seventy pairs. Who else have you given them to? Have you ever given any to your relatives?

BLANDON: No, sir.

LIPMAN: Sure? Ever give any to your neighbors?

BLANDON: No, sir.

LIPMAN: Think about that. Don't say no until you think about it. I don't want to find out later that you haven't told me the truth.

8:40 A.M.

LIPMAN: Come in please, Mr. Fischer. Eddie White here has
　　been working for you for about four years. He took a couple
　　of pairs of pants when he wanted them, not a big deal. And
　　he had some help getting them out, right, Eddie?

WHITE: Yes, sir.

LIPMAN: Have you ever driven a truck?

WHITE: No, sir.

LIPMAN: In three and a half years, that's 175 weeks, if you only
　　took two pairs a week, that's about 350 pair. Did you think
　　anything was wrong when you did that?

WHITE: I don't think it was that many.

LIPMAN: How many people are involved with you in this steal-
　　ing?

WHITE: Just myself and Blandon.

LIPMAN: That's all? You mean you didn't put any into a box like
　　the others?

WHITE: No, sir.

LIPMAN: How many of these pants have you sold?

WHITE: Not any.

LIPMAN: Where did you go to college?

WHITE: Waco College.

LIPMAN: How come you quit after two and a half years?

WHITE: I got two children.

LIPMAN: Let's estimate how many pants you got in the last year.

WHITE: I'd say about fifteen pairs in three years' time.

LIPMAN: How many do you have at home?

WHITE: About fifteen.

LIPMAN: You're not making any sense. We're going to have to
　　polygraph you to double check that.

WHITE: Yes, sir.

LIPMAN: Only fifteen pairs in three years. That's about a pair every two and a half months. You got a couple of pairs last Friday. What did you do with those pairs? Have you worn them?

WHITE: No, sir.

LIPMAN: Are they home? What do you think about stealing? Do you look on it as stealing when you take a pair of pants like that?

WHITE: I don't know.

LIPMAN: But you wouldn't walk in and hold up a store . . .

WHITE: Oh, no, no.

LIPMAN: But it doesn't seem to bother you or anybody else here to steal the merchandise.

WHITE: Well, it bothers you if you think about it. You get to thinking and you think, "Maybe I shouldn't be doing this."

LIPMAN: What percentage do you think are stealing here? Twenty-five percent? Fifty percent? A hundred percent?

WHITE: I don't know.

LIPMAN: Don't you think those women might be walking out with pants in their handbags?

WHITE: It's a good possibility.

So we polygraphed White about those fifteen pairs he had stolen, and the figure came out between seventy-five and a hundred.

We're back at the hotel now, about to have lunch. The city detectives went away with four of those punks.

I interrogated seven of the twenty or so thieves Sterling had reported and got confessions from all of them. About ten o'clock this morning I went to see Mr. Roach, the boss here, and a detective Braddock was there from downtown to arrest these guys as soon as I had finished with them. I'm all for arresting fences or wholesalers outside who might be buying this stuff, but I don't see the point of arresting these punks. And in this case we were unable to develop any such criminals. It may be that here in Waco they don't exist. We'd have to put in several more agents to find out, and the company doesn't want to spend that kind of money.

The ones I caught were not hardened criminals; they stole because the company made it easy for them and because everyone else in the plant, and in today's society as a whole, is doing the same damn thing. These guys just wanted to style up without spending any money.

One of those punks said to me, "The company doesn't pay anything, so you take pants instead of pay."

I asked another of them if he thought stealing pants was wrong, and he said, "If I did, I wouldn't be doing it."

What has happened to America?

And agent Sterling said about Hearn, that good-looking kid with the decayed front teeth, "If this were a more secure plant, I doubt if Hearn would have got started, but once he was introduced to it, he really loved it."

I found out that people were stealing pants that weren't yet on the market—they'd take home pants they didn't dare wear, and they'd keep going into a certain store downtown waiting to see that style appear on the shelves so they could start wearing their loot.

What does any punk do with seventy pairs of pants in his closet?

One of the punks said to me: "Are you going to check those women, because every single one of them is doing it."

The charges against the four boys who were arrested will probably be dropped. Trials are too expensive to make it worth the company's while. Besides, it would be hard to find a jury that would convict such clean-cut American boys for stealing a few thousand dollars worth of pants. You see, juries today don't really think stealing is wrong either.

The other twenty or so guys whom Sterling reported will be fired.

The rest of the 250 people in that one plant will go on working there even though the chemical which puts those permanent presses in your pants makes their eyes water. I don't know how anyone can work in constant contact with those chemicals. Mr. Fischer tells me the people get used to it after a couple of days.

And unless controls are put in, the stealing will go on. I've referred Fischer to my son Ira, because Guardsmark would help him.

Waco, Texas. Middle America. Stealing.

You know, Sterling liked that town a lot, partly because he got married there. He also said it was a town almost without prejudice. He said that the only prejudice he saw in Waco was between the cowboys and the hippies.

So the country is making progress in some things.

Before the Waco case, Sterling had worked for me in two meat packing plants, one of them in Chicago, the other in Atlanta, and also in a major department store. He's the son of an Air Force Lieutenant Colonel, and he has two and a half years of college. He was a very quiet, introverted type when he came to me. This job has helped bring him out of his shell.

A few weeks after he came on this job here in Waco, he met this Laura Lovegooding. She is 19. Within a few days he told her he was an undercover agent working for me, which he wasn't supposed to do, and a few weeks after that they got married. I didn't know he had got married at first, but I knew something had come into his life, because he began to be late with his reports. He had other things to do, you understand, besides writing his reports. Shortly after that he told me he was quitting me. He would finish this assignment, then he planned to move with Laura out to the northwest. He wants to run a ski lift in Montana. He doesn't want anything more to do with crime.

Today, between interrogations, I was trying to talk him into staying with me. He's a good boy. One of the very best. He believes in the old fashioned virtues I was brought up to believe in, such as the fact that stealing is wrong. He and I are among the very few in America today who do believe that, apparently.

People say America was built on moral principles. Not true. This country's always been an immoral society. It was a wilderness; it had no rules. People just went in and took what they had the force to take. They killed anyone who got in their way, especially if the victims could be called savages. The country was built up on land speculation and gold and silver strikes—it was built on greed to get that gold. People would do anything to get money, and that's how things really got rolling. The gold-strike mentality is still part of this country. No one wants to work hard all his life. Everyone is hoping and dreaming of the one big sale, the one big deal—the big payoff, the jackpot. If offered a dishonest shot at that jackpot, too many Americans would grab it with no second thoughts.

To control immorality it was necessary to have guns for protection. The country grew up under a law of guns, and we still have guns everywhere.

There always was a strong religious streak too, and that helped to tame things down, but religion is on the way out today, so what do we have? We have all these people stealing who don't even really think it's wrong to steal. We have people building and selling shoddy goods, which is just another way of stealing, and they think that's okay as long as you turn a profit. The jackpot mentality again. Everybody's motivated by greed, while all around us the church population is going down all the time. Look around at all the broken families, all the kids growing up without going to church. I think it's important that a kid goes to church until he's 10 or 15 years old. By that time he's been inculcated with what religion means—it doesn't make any difference what religion he follows, because basically they all follow the same thinking. By that time he's been inculcated with the thought of fear.

Today the only time the churches are filled up is on Easter or Yom Kippur or Christmas. Week after week people don't go to their church at all. Church doesn't mean anything to them. If their parents don't go the children don't go. Or the parents satisfy themselves by sending the kids to Sunday School. That's great. But the children see that church is not important enough for the parents to go and so the children don't think much of it either. They go because they have to go. They're not getting anything out of it. They're not getting any strong concept of right and wrong, or morality.

Today, how many people sit and read the Bible at home? With their parents, like they did in the olden days? You don't find much of that any more. How many times do you see a Bible lying in the house and you can look at that Bible and see it's never been opened? You can tell that nobody ever reads it? It's just there. For what purpose, no one knows, really.

I think our society today, with this divorce rate the way it is, is falling apart. There is a man I know well. Much to my surprise, last week his wife sued for divorce. Been married 15 years. A talented man. A good man, a church-going man. They're getting a divorce. They're not stopping to consider two children 9 and 11 years old, and what's going to happen to those children.

I talked to this man and told him that I thought it wrong. He came back with, "You can't live in a house where there isn't any love. The children sense that."

I don't go along with that theory. I think it's their obligation to make some sacrifice, to stay together until their kids are of college age. That's just a few years more, five or eight more years to wait.

But they are selfish. One of them may have had a lover.

Maybe there was more love elsewhere, their animal instincts were satisfied better elsewhere, the chemistry was better elsewhere. But that's a sacrifice I think should be made. I don't think sex is everything in marriage. Sex is very, very important, it's a must, but I don't think it's everything.

People say to me, "To be mixed up with thieves all the time —doesn't that make you terribly cynical?"

Yeah, it makes me cynical.

I remember that time in Chicago at the Acme Packing Company. After Midnight Shadow had been fired, I saw him outside with the union business agent. I heard this union guy promise to get Shadow another job by Monday so he could steal somewhere else. It's so goddam stinking—

Thieves today don't even wait. Two or three weeks after one gang gets caught, it starts all over again in the same place. We broke this Department Store case in Dallas a while back, and I talked the management into keeping somebody in there year round—gave them a special rate. We put a girl in there; nothing happened for about three or four weeks. Then it started up again—not as much, not as great a volume, but people started taking out garments again. And these garments sell for $50 to $75 each. I broke that case a second time and then left the female agent in there and sent a male agent to work outside. Now I'm about to go into that same store to break that case once again—three times in a year and a half. That's a perfect example of what's going on in this country today. Everybody's stealing there. I sometimes think everybody's stealing everywhere.

Most people today don't know the difference between what is wrong and what is not wrong. People steal a dress. People lie just a little. We called an agent in the other day and told him he had been exaggerating his reports. He didn't understand the difference.

Honesty doesn't mean anything. People know they're not

going to be arrested for lying or for stealing a dress. If they know that people can bomb buildings, can tear up streets, can do any damn thing they want, and get only a slap on the wrist, they know that nothing much is going to happen if they take a dress. How are you going to prevent this? How are you going to change this world? The American people take for granted that the white-collar worker or the blue-collar worker is stupid and that stealing is not important.

Here's a girl like Angela Davis, who is alleged to be part of an operation to kill a judge, and all those people are going to bat for her to raise some money, so what the hell if somebody did steal a case of dresses? Or a case of shoes? There are no values anymore. Nobody has any values. Absolutely none. I can remember the days when if I caught a guy stealing $100—he would break down and cry and feel so bad about it. And today I catch a guy who'll admit $20,000 and he doesn't shed a tear. Why? Of course there are still some that do, but most of them —nothing, nothing.

Am I ashamed of America? What's going on here is going on all over the world. We only see what's in front of us. As long as you have people who covet things, you're going to have stealing. That's the way people are. There must have been some reason for biblical injunctions against covetousness.

Look, I'm just one private investigator. My firm is by no means the biggest. This book represents only part of our case load for one three-month period. Nothing particularly unusual —unusual to me, that is—happened during those three months. It was all distressingly normal.

What I have shown you is not the whole picture—it's just a corner of it. You can supply the rest yourself. Multiply the factories I have gone into, the confessions I have extracted, the larceny I have uncovered by any number you care to. I don't think you'd be exaggerating anything.

Do you realize how many sides of beef, how many kitchenette sets, how many garments are being stolen right this
minute? Do you realize what is going on in this country today?

7. Stealing Is
Big Business

Often a client will state that he's losing a great deal of merchandise, although he can't imagine how. Sometimes he has some definite leads. In any case, generally speaking, the most vulnerable areas in a plant are shipping and receiving. That's where I look first. Not that I invariably place my undercover man there at once. It's a good idea to place a new agent in an area other than the most vulnerable one for at least a two- or three-week period, which is known as an orientation period—orientation for the thieves. It lets them get used to the agent's presence without any suspicions being aroused. After a time the agent becomes part of the scenery. He is then moved into the vulnerable area. This is usually very productive.

Many firms want to know why I decide to put someone in the receiving area. Goods only arrive there, they think; but surprisingly enough, big thefts often occur while vendors are supposedly delivering merchandise. It takes about one minute or less for a forklift to pick up a pallet of merchandise—which may have arrived only seconds before—and to put it into the vendor's empty truck and out she goes. The vendor makes two profits, one for delivering a legitimate load of goods and one for stealing a load either diverted to receiving or just delivered there legitimately by someone else.

There are two types of stealing: case loads which go out by truck or stolen parcels that an employee might toss over the fence and come back for later. I'm talking here about the first type. For that I always start with the two key places, shipping and receiving. The merchandise gets out via a chain of operations. There has to be a man who picks it out and gets it to the packer, who perhaps marks the box in a certain way so that the shipping clerk gets it on the proper truck. There must be a chain of operations in order to steal in any volume. All I have to do to interrupt this chain at any point is find out how the merchandise flows. Where does it start, and where does it leave the plant? If there's no way out via the shipping department— perhaps because there are too many controls there—then it is probably going out through receiving.

Another place I immediately check out when surveying a client's plant is the mail room. The mail room area is very vulnerable. Over and over again I catch employees who have fallen into the habit of mailing packages of company merchandise to themselves. Usually they use the company stamps to do it too.

So I ask who is in charge of the mail room. Is there a registry book and someone to write down what comes into the mail room and what goes out? A lot of firms have such controls, but many do not. Who has the right to bring stuff to the mail room, and what sort of invoices must he show?

Of course, controls cost money and too many firms prefer to take a calculated risk. Maybe so-and-so will not steal. A lot of stealing, and particularly mail room stealing, could be controlled if companies would spend a little money.

I suppose you think that mail room thieves invariably send the stolen merchandise to a dummy address. Not true. Many of them are brazen enough to mail these goods to their home address. They are convinced that their employer is not paying any attention. If the employer is that stupid, they have nothing but contempt for him, so they send the stuff right out to their own homes, and it is still arriving in the mail when I go out to look for it.

A simple thing like a garbage disposal may prove to be an outlet for stolen merchandise. That's another place I look at quickly. Often there is so much rubbish lying around the incinerator that goods are stashed there, and of course plenty of merchandise goes out on garbage trucks. I'll tell you how cruel some of these guys are. They leave the stuff near the incinerator, and if a supervisor should come snooping around, if they fear they might get caught, they take the merchandise, the live merchandise and burn it up. That happened recently in a distribution plant in Texas. There was a series of conveyor belts moving the goods around the plant, and the thieves were working both floors. A guy on the second floor would send the goods down to the first floor on a belt, and the first-floor guy, if the coast was clear, would take the goods off and stash them. If the coast was not clear, if someone happened to be watching him, he would toss the goods onto another belt leading straight into the incinerator.

Here are ten points that I try to make clear to the client.

1. For reasons of tact, I usually make this point last, not first, though it is the most important control that a client can put in. Many of the owners and managers who call me in don't pay their employees enough, and that invites stealing. Of course, there are employees you could pay three times as much and they'd still steal; but generally speaking less stealing goes on in plants where people are overpaid than in plants where they are underpaid. You've got to make an employee feel that his job is worth keeping, that he can't earn more elsewhere.

So control number one, I tell my clients, is to pay a good wage. I make a lot of clients angry by saying this, and some tell me to my face that they prefer to accept the existing rate of theft, that they will simply make up the loss out of employee paychecks; for as long as the stealing goes on, nobody gets a raise.

I then point out that these days there is a new kind of security risk abroad in the land. I suppose you would call it vandalism. People get angry at the boss and deliberately ruin expensive machinery or deliberately flaw vast quantities of the product. Only recently a large catering company, one of the largest in the United States, called me in. The usual story, profits way down. They thought a ring of employees was looting the place, but I couldn't uncover this ring.

What I did find was one disgruntled female employee who was purposely altering the payroll records so that all the checks were made out in higher amounts. Everybody got a raise. First, no employee thanked management for this raise; and second, modern machine-printed checks are so impersonal and so complicated that these errors were not that obvious. Meanwhile, the company was losing heavily. After making a field investigation that led nowhere, I switched to the disgruntled-employee theory, discovered the altered payroll, and then zeroed in on this one woman.

It pays to pay well.

2. A one-story factory is safer than a factory with multiple levels because there are fewer staircases, closets, and corners where merchandise can be stashed. The first job of the thief, after all, is to divert merchandise, to remove it from the normal flow of traffic. This means that it must be hidden for a time. I also tell clients to keep their plants in order—no piles of rubbish or rejects or boxes, no disused machines with tarpaulins on them, no unlocked empty drawers. In short, there should be no place where stolen goods can be hidden.

3. Paperwork must be carefully examined and checked at all stages so that invoices can't be stolen or altered. I tell clients to

go over their paperwork system most carefully, and if they find any flaws or holes, to close them up.

4. Employees' cars should not be parked close to the department store or plant. They should be parked no closer than fifty feet away, with no usable cover between the plant doors and the cars, so that employees can't run out to their cars several times a day with parcels of stolen merchandise, and, hidden among the cars, stash stuff in their trunks. Also, there should be a guard—or if it's a big plant, several guards—patrolling that no-man's-land all day. If you don't like Guardsmark, use some other service, but get a guard. What the guard keeps from disappearing into employees' cars each month will more than pay his salary.

5. Female employees must not be allowed to keep their handbags next to them at work. Lockers that lock must be provided for them. Merchandise has a way of disappearing into those handbags, and once the latch is closed you need a search warrant to get it open again. Similarly, there should be no pockets on the ladies' dresses or smocks. There should be no pockets in men's clothes either, but unfortunately men's clothes are not made that way, and the unions would scream if you tried to enforce such a regulation. What I'm saying is that all employees ought to wear uniforms. Sounds like slavery, doesn't it? But if the stealing goes on much longer at the current pace, that's what will happen, and what does this say about freedom in America?

Even uniforms would control stealing only a little, not end it. People determined to steal would wrap the goods around their bodies and, pockets or no pockets, walk out with it, as we've seen.

6. Whether the place is open or closed at night, bright lights should blaze all around the perimeter so that no one can enter or leave without fear of detection. Many's the employee who

has hidden in the factory after closing time and left in the middle of the night with all he could carry.

7. Who has the keys to the place? Can "trusted" people come back for merchandise at night? Is somebody not locking a door he's supposed to lock, and is this done by accident or for his own purposes? We've also had cases where a manager or supervisor would come back at night with a girlfriend and have a good time, and afterwards give her an armload of merchandise to take home with her. So key control is very important.

8. Everyone entering or leaving should have an identification card. Vehicles must be checked both entering and leaving. A simple thing like checking outgoing trucks makes it impossible for, say, a soft drink truck bound for the catering department to go out with a load of stolen goods.

9. Keep surplus doors locked. If only two need to be open to handle normal traffic, then bolt up the rest. No one can watch fifteen or twenty open doors, and to put a guard on each one would be too expensive. Lock them up tightly. I realize that some fire laws demand that many or all doors be openable in case of fire; if this is the case in your plant, then invest in alarm-type doors. Let a nice loud siren go off if a thief tries to go out on the sly. Are such doors too expensive? They are cheaper than the goods that go out unlocked doors. Or maybe you need to keep them all open in hot weather as ventilation. In that case, invest in air-conditioning and lock them up tightly. Air-conditioning, no matter how expensive, will cost you less money than unlocked doors.

10. You must safeguard everything of value that thieves could possibly remove, not just obvious items. Hospitals are plagued with thefts today, as I've said. Administrators call me in and tell me about missing drugs and about the systematic theft of linens. I tell them that their dietary departments are probably getting looted too, and they look at me stunned. Of

course, there is a ready market for hospital drugs and for sheets, pillowcases, and towels as well, and so much of this stuff comes and goes that administrators can't keep track of it all. But hospital employees steal a great deal of food also. The dietary departments suffer tremendous losses because most of their employees—most, I said—take home some food every day, and some take home enough for dinner for their entire families every day. Why do you think hospitals are so expensive? Do you think theft has nothing to do with it?

Not long ago employees in the dietary department of one of the nation's largest hospitals admitted to me theft of food items in excess of $50,000 over a period of four years. Since the dietary area was not used at night, they were able to carry out merchandise and place it in their autos for later sale to a grocery store. I put three of my undercover agents in that place and told them the stealing probably occurred at night. They quickly obtained the evidence I needed. Under interrogation, the employees admitted these thefts, each one trying to lay most of the blame on the others.

There are many reasons why employees steal. Among them are liquor, sex, gambling, extravagant living, and the increase in narcotics addiction. Drugs are a growing problem for management. Many employees who might not have stolen ten years ago are today hooked on heroin. Because they still consider themselves honest, they will steal only enough to take care of their habits for each day. On the other hand, there are many who start in this manner but soon get reckless and begin to push drugs on other employees in the plant; they actually get other employees addicted in order to create a market in the plant. The profit they make pushing drugs enables them to cut down on their own thefts.

But the number one reason why people steal is temptation. If, in the course of his work, the employee is faced with an opportunity to steal, he will steal in most cases. If the internal safeguards are poor, something should be done about it. These security flaws are often inadvertent and unknown to management. I see most of them at once, and a professional undercover agent with a watchful eye can catch even the trickiest security hazards in a very short time. Sometimes a flaw is deeply engrained into a method of operation so that it is not noticeable to someone close to the scene.

Many companies are reluctant to use undercover agents because they do not want to spy on their employees. However, my experience has unfortunately shown that it is the most trusted employee who is frequently tempted to steal. The long-time employee knows the company and its flaws best, and it may take an undercover agent, operating under the guise of a "fellow worker," to catch him.

Industrial thefts are escalating at the rate of 15–20 per cent; estimates in dollar volume range from $3 billion to $15 billion a year.

Employees need opportunity to commit theft. When I go into a plant where theft is suspected, the first thing I tell management is that they must structure the environment so that the opportunity to commit theft will be diminished. Too many good employees have become hardened thieves because the temptation was so great and the system so lax that they took advantage of it. Enough controls can be put into effect so that at least a percentage of would-be thieves will be discouraged from stealing.

After reading this book, one gets the impression that everybody in America is stealing, and this is partially true. I would say that a minimum of half the people who work in industry, whether in plants or in offices, actually steal, even if they take only pencils or notepaper home for their kids. This is petty theft. But of the 50 percent who steal, half of them—25 percent of the nation's work force—steal important items for their own personal use and benefit. Probably 5–8 percent of all workers steal in volume.

What sort of profile does the modern thief have? All right, some are punks and some are executives, but the average company thief is a married man, has two or three children, lives in a fairly good community, plays bridge with his neighbors, goes to church regularly, is well thought of by his boss. He is highly trusted and a good worker, one of the best in the plant. That's why he can steal so much over such long periods and why it's so hard to discover his identity.

America's factory owners need to know who's stealing their goods. The survival of the American way of life depends on it. Who's stealing raw materials and tools; who's stealing man-hours? How much goofing off is there among the employees? Are time cards being faked and payrolls padded? Are purchasing agents getting kickbacks? The most economical way to find these things out is to place an undercover agent in the plant.

I wish we lived in a society where no undercover agents were necessary. I wish there were no need for detectives like me. I wish no one stole or that only a limited number of warped individuals stole. Unfortunately, our society just isn't this way and America's national pastime today is not baseball, it is theft.

73 74 75 10 9 8 7 6 5 4 3 2 1